Living with Others

Biodiversity around us

M.A. HAQUE

PUBLICATIONS DIVISION
MINISTRY OF INFORMATION AND BROADCASTING
GOVERNMENT OF INDIA

2013 (Saka 1934)
First Reprint: November 2023 (*Saka 1945*)

PD ISBN: 978-81-19936-19-9
BN F&F-ENG-REP-180-2023-24

Price ₹ 190.00

Published by : The Director General, Publications Division, Ministry of Information and Broadcasting, Government of India, Soochna Bhawan, C.G.O. Complex, Lodhi Road, New Delhi-110003

http/www.publicationsdivision.nic.in

Editing : S. Manjula
Cover Design : Asha Saxena.

Sales Centres : • Book Gallery, Soochna Bhawan, C.G.O. Complex, Lodhi Road, **New Delhi**-110003 • 701, B-Wing, Kendriya Sadan, Belapur, **Navi Mumbai**-400614 • 8, Esplanade East, **Kolkata**-700069 • 'A' Wing, Rajaji Bhawan, Besant Nagar, **Chennai**-600090 • Press Road, Near Govt. Press, **Thiruvananthapuram**-695001 • Room No. 204, 2nd Floor, C.G.O. Towers, Kavadiguda, **Hyderabad**-500080 • 1st Floor, 'F' Wing, Kendriya Sadan, Koramangala, **Bengaluru**-560034 • Bihar State Co-operative Bank Building, Ashoka Rajpath, **Patna**-800004 • Hall No.1, 2nd Floor, Kendriya Bhawan, Sector-H, Aliganj, **Lucknow**-226024.

Typeset by: **Compudata Services,** New Delhi - 110020

Printed at : VIBA Press Pvt. Ltd., C66/3, Okhla Industrial Area, Ph-II, New Delhi-110020

Contents

Contents

CHAPTER 1

Introduction

The year 2010 was declared by the UN (United Nations) as "The International Year of Biodiversity". Obviously, the purpose behind this move was to attract the attention of the world towards the biodiversity present on the Earth. The United Nations started the tradition of associating a particular year with a particular theme in 1959. Since 1959 the UN has regularly designated International Years. The purpose is obvious. By assigning a theme to a whole year, attention of the entire world can be drawn towards the issue which can encourage international action to address concerns relating to the issue which is of global importance and ramifications. This way, year after year important issues have been brought to focus by the United Nations. But it is not so that every year since 1959 has been designated so. Certain years have been left out deliberately taking into account fiscal reasons and also to avoid trivialization of the exercise.1959 was celebrated as the "World refugee Year", 1965 was declared as "International Cooperation Year", 1998 was declared as the "International Year of Ocean". The 2002 was declared as the "International Year of Mountains", 2003 was declared as the "International Year of Freshwater", 2006 was the "International Year of Deserts and Desertification", 2009 was celebrated as the "International Year of Natural Fibres". While 2011 was celebrated as the "International Year of Forests".

Following the same tradition during the year 2010 biodiversity continued to be in focus and various functions and programmes were organized all over the world to highlight the status of biodiversity, its value and threats faced by it. The activities also highlighted the possible actions which can conserve biodiversity on a global scale. Various programmes focussed on different facets of biodiversity. The concluding function was held in Japan in the city of Kanazawa. The celebration focussed on the achievements of the International Year of Biodiversity. Also, the occasion was used for contribution to the launch of the "International Year of Forests" i.e. The main goals of the International Year was of Biodiversity were to:

- Enhance public awareness of the importance of conserving biodiversity and of the underlying threats to biodiversity
- Raise awareness of the accomplishments to save biodiversity that have already been realized by communities and governments
- Promote innovative solutions to reduce the threats to biodiversity

- Encourage individuals, organizations and governments to take immediate steps to halt biodiversity loss
- Start dialogue between stakeholders for the steps to be taken in the post-2010 period.

At this point the question that arises is why the UN had to designate a year for biodiversity? In this regard it is important to understand Earth is a part of the larger solar system. If we look at the diagram of the solar system, it is located at the third position from Sun. In all, there are eight planets in the solar system and Earth is the largest one with highest mass and maximum density among the four planets which are called the terrestrial planets. These are Mercury, Venus, Earth and Mars. These planets are primarily made of silicate rocks. Earth is quite often called the Blue Planet as well. Reason is that the three fourth of the surface of Earth is covered by water mainly in the form of oceans and seas. Presence of water on the surface of Earth is a unique feature of Earth. On looking from the space the area looks blue in colour. If we take into account the quantity of water present in the oceans, it works out to about 1.35×10^{18} metric tons. In terms of volume it is about 1.38×10^{9} cubic km. Most of the water present on Earth (about 97.5%) is saline. The rest i.e. about 2.5% is fresh water. In this regard it is important to note that most of the requirements for the living organisms and activities on the land part of Earth are met from fresh water. But all the fresh water present on Earth is not available. For example, about 70% of the fresh water is in the form of ice and a certain percentage of the fresh water is in deep rocks. As such these are not readily utilizable.

The oceans carry a heavy load of salts. About 3.5% of the ocean mass is due to the salts present there. These salts reached there either on account of volcanic activities or from igneous rocks. On account of the presence of salts in the sea water, there is salinity which makes sea water different from water. This differentiates the oceans as a habitat from water habitats like rivers, lakes, ponds, reservoirs etc. In addition to the salts, sea water holds large quantities of dissolved atmospheric gases. These gases are utilized by organisms living in the water for their activities. Water present in the oceans plays important role in deciding the Earth's climate as well. The oceans can store huge quantity of heat and changes in the pattern of ocean temperature can lead to changes in the weather conditions in different parts of Earth.

Water in liquid form is known to exist only on Earth. This water is responsible for life on Earth. There is no organism which does not contain water and which can survive without water. Some of the organisms may contain up to 95% or even more of water in terms of mass. Our own body which consists of various types of tissues including the hard bones consists of about 70% water. Water is regularly lost from the body of the organisms living outside water in liquid form or as vapour causing deficit of water in the body. This is the reason that all such organisms need to absorb water on regular basis. Larger animals do so by drinking water. Plants, microbes, and smaller animals satisfy their need by absorbing it through their body surface.

Earth is known to interact with various objects in the outer space, sun and moon included. Earth is not stationary. It moves around the sun and simultaneously it rotates on its own axis too. It completes its rotation around the sun in the same time when it completes its rotation on its axis 366.26 times. The time required to complete the rotation is 365.26 solar days. This is the reason why after every four years we have a leap year in our calendar. The solar calendar consists of 365 days. After every four year one day is added to February to compensate for the 0.26 extra day in the solar year. An important fact is that the axis of rotation of the Earth is not straight. It is tilted by 23.4° away from the vertical. This tilt is responsible for the seasonal variations that we experience on the Earth. Moon is the only known satellite which orbits around the Earth. Presence of the Moon is responsible for the tides that are generated in the oceans. Moon is also responsible for gradual slowing down of the rotation of the Earth. But it is an extremely slow process and we need not worry about it.

Earth is made of a thick outer solid layer which is called the mantle. Under the mantle there is a liquid layer called outer core and the inner most of the Earth is again solid. It is called inner core and it is mainly made of iron. The outermost or uppermost layer of the Earth is called the pedosphere. This is the part of Earth with which we regularly interact. It is composed of soil and we know that soil is the basis of all vegetation and agriculture. The soil provides support for anchorage to the plants. It is the storehouse of nutrients which are absorbed by plants and soil is the layer where water is stored to be absorbed by plants. From the plants the food materials and the nutrients reach the animal world including humans. A large fraction of water also reaches the animal body with the food obtained from plants. This is the reason that soil is considered very important for life on Earth and its degradation or loss is not good for the living organisms.

Soil is formed due to breaking of the rocks into smaller pieces. Breaking of the rocks takes place due to chemical processes and environmental changes on Earth's surface. The process is generally called weathering or erosion. Once formed the soil is quite different from the parent rock or rocks from which it is formed. Reason is that soil does not consist of only the mineral particles coming from the rocks. The impact of water, atmosphere and living organisms play an important role in formation of soil and in determining its properties. Finally, it becomes a mixture of mineral materials derived from the rocks and organic matter coming from the living organisms. An important feature is soil has pore spaces between the particles. The pore spaces are responsible for keeping the soil porous and light. These pores hold water and air as well. The same water is utilized by plants for their survival. The water present in soil pores dissolves nutrients and other materials and helps in their absorption by plants. Air present in the pore spaces provides oxygen to the underground portions of plants. This is why very compact soil is not good for growth of plants. Farmers keep the soil porous by ploughing the land before seeding and by regular digging and turning it while the plants are growing.

If we finally come to the human race, we find that the mineral resources and living organisms provide various types of resources and support to the human population. We cannot think of survival without these resources. Another important issue is that although the Earth is politically divided into large number of nations and countries in terms of environment it is not possible to find such demarcation. Undoubtedly there are *certain environmental issues which are of local nature. But there are other issues which* affect the entire human race directly or indirectly. Well known examples are the depletion of ozone layer, greenhouse effect and climate change etc. In certain conditions even pollution of air and water become international issues. Also, biodiversity is now recognized as an international issue. Reason is that the biological resources present in any part of the may prove useful for the entire humanity either directly or indirectly. For example, discovery of an organism in any part of the world, which may help in controlling or curing certain disease, will in the long run benefit the entire human race. Similarly, discovery of some new crop variety with better productivity may immediately give benefit to those who discover the new crop variety. But in the long run the benefit is likely to spread to other parts of the world. This is the reason that if the biological resources are lost in any part of the Earth, it is considered a loss for the entire humanity. Taking the same into account the United Nations declared 2010 as the International Year of Biodiversity. The idea was to involve people from all walks of life in safeguarding the biodiversity present on Earth. Reason is obvious. Biodiversity is vital for the survival and wellbeing of the present generation and future generations. This will provide opportunity to people in general to appreciate the importance of biodiversity in our lives, the risks being faced by biodiversity, factors responsible for those risks and the role each one of us can play in eliminating or reducing the risks to the biodiversity.

We need to realize that India is quite rich in terms of biodiversity. There are various factors responsible for this. About 21% of the geographical area of the country is classified as forests. About 2.54% of the geographical area is covered by Very Dense Forest (VDF), about 9.7% is under Medium Density Forest (MDF) and about 8.77% is under Open Forest (OF). Trees outside the forests occupy about 2.82% of the land area. In a way it seems to be quite a comfortable position. However, if we go into the recent past we find that we have lost quite substantial portion of the forests. At the beginning of the 20th century about 40% of India's geographical area was under high quality forest. Thus it is obvious that during the last one century the country lost about half of the forest area. Still there are different types of forests present in different parts of the country. In terms of agriculture as well India supports 21 distinct agro-ecosystems. Different types of crops are grown in the country and various types of cropping patterns are followed. Biogeographically, the country shows a wide scale of variation. That is the reason that India consists of ten bio-geographic zones. These are: Coasts, Deccan Peninsula, Desert Zone, Gangetic Plains, Himalayan Zone, Islands, North-East Zone, Semi-arid Zone and Trans Himalayan Zone.

Conventional varieties of seeds on display to raise awareness about shrinking varieties of crops

Natural forest shrinking in Western Ghats due to expansion of agriculture

A large tree converted into a temple

A neglected pond attached to a temple – dirty and full of algae

Mangrove seedlings for plantation

This richness of India's biodiversity brings responsibilities too. The biodiversity must be used only in a sustainable manner. That will help maintain the resource base. Also, we need to conserve the biodiversity for future. Historically, India had a strong tradition of attaching reverence to habitats like forests, rivers, lakes, ponds etc. and also to plants and animals. The reverence continues even now. The same may be on account of religious belief, social and cultural traditions, and quite often on account of fear and superstition. In the past natural resources received protection against large scale plunder and destruction on account of this reverence. But during last five or six decades there have been large scale changes in lifestyle in the country. There is growing materialism. Simultaneous social and community traditions have become weak. Result is that the communities which traditionally provided protection to forests, wildlife, wild plants, water bodies etc. have become unconcerned towards these resources. That was one of the important reasons why the country lost large chunks of forests, water bodies and other natural habitats etc. Water bodies like ponds, lakes, rivers also suffered on account of pollution, growth of weeds, eutrophication etc. A large number of the natural habitats have vanished completely. On account of this various plants and animals came under threat and a number of them became extinct.

Parallel to this a positive development has taken place. Till about two decades back, people in general were rarely concerned about the natural habitats. Also, the flora and fauna present in them were not considered of any value. This kind of lack of concern resulted in the complete extermination of cheetah from India. In 1947 last three cheetahs were killed. From then onwards there is no cheetah in the country in the wild. Several species of large animals like tigers, lions, elephants, rhinos etc. have been drastically reduced in number and their habitats have been shrinking continuously. During last one or two decades awareness towards environment has increased. Several factors are responsible for the same. One important reason has been that natural disasters like floods, drought, cyclones, landslides, instability of weather and climate etc. have increased. People now realize that these are directly or indirectly linked to degradation the environment. People are trying to rediscover the age old traditions and rituals related to protection and conservation of the environment. Also, people are raising their voice to impress upon the government to take action aimed towards protection of the environment. Declaration of biodiversity rich areas as protected areas is one of such initiative. Large areas of forests, wetlands, coastal belts, mountain tracts, desert ecosystems and other biodiversity rich areas have been brought under the purview of protected areas network. National Biodiversity Authority has been constituted by the government with its headquarters at Chennai. Similar authorities are being established at state level. The initiative is to percolate to village level by way of Village Level Biodiversity Committees. These organizations will be responsible for conservation and sustainable utilization of the rich biodiversity spread in the country.

Proper cataloguing of the country's biodiversity is essential to protect it. Large areas of the country are unexplored and information about several groups of organisms is incomplete. Now steps are in place to reach the goal of complete cataloguing and documentation of India's biodiversity. Organizations like Botanical Survey of India (BSI), Zoological Survey of India (ZSI) are involved in the exercise. Additionally, numbers of universities, colleges, other educational institutions, government organizations, NGOs etc. are working to achieve the goal. But on account of the size of the country, lack of manpower and infrastructure, it may be difficult to complete the job in near future. Hence, steps are being taken on the one hand to conserve biodiversity and on the other hand to allow sustainable utilization of biodiversity.

In the subsequent chapters in this book we will discuss about the classification of biodiversity, richness of biodiversity on the Earth, with special reference to India. We will also discuss about value of biodiversity in day to day life and also in economy and industry, methods underway to conserve the biodiversity etc. The purpose is to make the readers better aware of various avenues of biodiversity so that they may also contribute to its conservation.

CHAPTER 2

Knowing Biodiversity

We are aware of the fact that Earth is the only planet in the entire solar system which is known to support life. Scientists have been continuously struggling for decades to collect evidence of existence of life on other planets. Till now concrete evidence has not been found to support the view that life as it is on the earth does exist on other planets. Hence, for the present we have to assume that Earth is the only place in the entire universe where life exists. If we look around us we find that large variety of plants, animals, microorganism exist in the environment. As far as microorganisms are concerned, the same may not be visible as such but their existence is evident. For example, if we leave the milk uncared, it gets spoiled on account of certain bacteria growing in the milk which cause souring. Similarly, when we prepare curd or yoghurt, we add some curd to the milk and leave it. The purpose of adding curd is to add a certain type of bacteria. Once added to the milk the bacteria multiply and due to their action the entire milk gets converted into curd or yoghurt. Similarly, we know that fermentation of molasses or sugar syrup produces alcohol. But it does not happen on its own. Yeast, a fungus, is responsible for fermentation of sugar syrup or molasses to produce alcohol. We see that the palm tree sap which collects during the night and is removed in the morning is sweet. The same sap which collects during the day and is taken out in the evening is not sweet and contains high percentage of alcohol. It is used for intoxication and is called toddy. Reason is that during night the temperature is low. The yeast cells are unable to perform fermentation. On the other hand during the day the temperature rises and yeast become active. Fermentation takes place on account of the activity of the yeast cells. Sugar present in the sap converts into alcohol making the sap an intoxicant. Same yeast cells cause fermentation in dough which results in fluffiness of breads. As these organisms grow better in warmer conditions formation of curd or yoghurt and fermentation of palm juice is faster in summer as compared to winter. In areas where temperature remains regularly low special arrangements have to be made to prepare curd or yoghurt.

Several types of diseases and infections are also caused by microorganisms. We cannot see those organisms with our naked eyes. But they are there in the environment and become infectious on entering our body. One common example of such diseases is tuberculosis (TB). Other examples are diarrhea, cholera, dysentery, malaria etc. The organisms causing these diseases too survive and proliferate better in warm environment. This is the reason that they occur more frequently in areas with warm climates. In other areas they appear more frequently during warmer seasons.

If we look at the origin of the term biodiversity, we find that it has been derived from two words: 'bios' meaning life and 'diversitas' which indicates variety. So, the term biodiversity stands for diversity of life forms. In practical terms biodiversity is the contracted form of Biological Diversity i.e. diversity of life forms. As such "biodiversity" can have many interpretations. But it is most commonly used to replace the more clearly defined and long established terms, species diversity and species richness. Biologists most often define biodiversity as the "totality of genes, species, and ecosystems of a region". As per experts the advantage of this particular definition is that it seems to describe most circumstances and present a unified view of the traditional three levels at which biological variety has been identified i.e.

1. genetic diversity
2. species diversity
3. ecosystem diversity

This multilevel conception is consistent with the early use of the expression "biological diversity". The 1992 United Nations Earth Summit in Rio de Janeiro defined "biological diversity" as "the variability among living organisms from all sources, including, 'inter alia', terrestrial, marine, and other aquatic ecosystems, and the ecological complexes of which they are a part, this includes diversity within species, between species and ecosystems". This is, in fact, the closest thing to a single legally accepted definition of biodiversity, since it is the definition adopted by the United Nations Convention on Biological Diversity.

Taking these into account the current textbook definition of "biodiversity" is "variation of life at all levels of biological organization".

Now let us understand in a little more detail what the term biodiversity stands for. When we talk of the entire Earth and we use the term Biodiversity we mean the entire range of different types of life forms which is present on the Earth. It ranges from the smallest organisms to the largest ones such as the tallest trees, huge animals like whales, elephants, giraffes, camels, rhinos etc. Obviously, it includes all plants, animals, microorganisms present on the Earth.

We are told by scientists that life started with very few simple organisms. It happened in water. Reason was that the atmosphere at the time was Ozone-free. As a result the ultraviolet (UV) rays coming from the sun could freely travel to Earth. We know that the UV rays are harmful for living organisms. Till the time this kind of situation continued life continued only under water. There the organisms could survive as UV rays do not penetrate water beyond a certain limit. Once, ozone layer was formed in the atmosphere and UV rays were stopped from reaching to Earth, life started to exist on land as well. This is the reason that during past several decades the human race has been worried about the depletion of ozone in the atmosphere. Ozone gas molecules form a thin layer in the stratosphere layer of the atmosphere. It plays very important role by stopping the UV rays coming from the sun towards Earth. During last few decades we have been using certain chemicals which travel upward in the atmosphere

Fishes in a sacred pond attached to a temple, an example of an ecosystem

Varieties of grain in a grocery store show biodiversity in daily use

A Haldi plant – representative of Indian biodiversity

Rare and endangered plants in a Botanical Garden, protecting biodiversity

and reach the stratosphere in due course of time. There these chemicals destroy the ozone molecules. That is the reason that these chemicals are commonly called ODS (ozone depleting substances). CFCs (Chlorofluorocarbons) form one such group. Now use of these chemicals is being reduced and wherever possible the use is being discontinued completely. For example modern refrigerators, air conditioners, water coolers etc. do not contain these chemicals. That is why these are labeled "ODS free". In this way we are trying to stop the process which could have led the Earth's environment to the stage when there was no ozone in the atmosphere. As a consequence life could exist only inside water.

We need to understand that the living organisms that we see today around us have not been around since life came into existence. Biodiversity present around us today is the result of 4 billion years of evolution. Estimates suggest that life on Earth has existed for the last about 4 billion years. It is further understood that till about 600 million years ago life on earth consisted of only single-celled organisms. Other types of organisms developed later.

Taking fossil records as evidence a group of scientists suggests that the last few million years has been the period of greatest biodiversity on the Earth during its entire history. However, there is another group of scientists with a different view point. That group is of the view that modern biodiversity is not much different from the biodiversity present on Earth 300 million years ago, suggesting that during the last about 300 million years there has not been any substantial change in the status of biodiversity on the Earth. On account of lack of knowledge estimates relating to the diversity of macroscopic species on global scale vary drastically. The range is from 2 million to 100 million species. However estimate of somewhere near 13–14 million is receiving wide support. Among these arthropods represent the largest group.

When we talk about biodiversity we keep ourselves out of it. Human being is also one group of living organisms. Human form a distinct species, Homo sapiens. It also depends on the resources present in the environment for its survival. Accordingly, human race is nothing but one component of the overall biodiversity present on the Earth. This view gets support if we look back into history on Earth. We find that till about few thousand years ago human being were almost at the same level as any other organism. They were collecting food from the environment. They did not have any capability to change the environment or influence the availability of food. Thus human race was simply a part of Earth's overall biodiversity. With passage of time the human race became more intelligent and learnt techniques to influence various processes on Earth and also it could alter the life forms present on the Earth. The human race encouraged certain organisms to proliferate while in case of others it retarded their growth and multiplication. In due course of time the human race became the most dominant species on the Earth and slowly, the concept of biodiversity developed into a form where only other living organisms were considered as components of the biodiversity. Virtually, human race acquired the status of being different and more importantly 'above' the other living organisms. As a result, we do not include human beings when we talk of biodiversity present on Earth. This system has its pitfalls. For example, when we consider ourselves above other organisms, a false notion of superiority percolates in our mind. We take it for granted that we have the right to use the other living organisms i.e. biodiversity present on Earth the way it suits us. This notion has resulted in overexploitation and misuse of biological resources. It also gives us the wrong notion that we have the right to eliminate organisms which we do not need or which are harmful in our opinion. Such activities on the part of humans have resulted in imbalances and degradation of the environment. For example, we have eliminated or are on the verge of eliminating large number of organisms which are otherwise useful to the environment. If we had continued to consider ourselves as part of the overall biodiversity, we would have been more concerned about the biodiversity in general. This kind of understanding, if it was there, could lead to positive developments and the kind of degradation the earth's biodiversity has been subjected to by us could have been avoided. However, in the present context we cannot deviate from the accepted definition and hence we have to exclude ourselves from the biodiversity present on Earth.

Scientists give the concept that with passage of time the process of evolution continued and it produced large variety of living organisms including microorganisms, plants and animals. During the process of evolution new types of organisms evolved and parallel to the same certain existing types disappeared. The natural process of disappearance of living organisms is called extinction. Thus the processes of evolution and extinction have been going on side by side. During certain period of time the process of extinction became fast resulting in disappearance of large varieties of living organisms. On the other hand the process of evolution or formation of new types of organisms has been going on at almost constant speed. This is the reason that in the history of Earth there have been certain events when Earth was almost without living organisms. Such events are called mass extinctions. But there have been no instances of "mass evolution". Evolution has always been a very slow process.

Living organisms, including humans, cannot live in isolation. All of them live in different ecosystems. There the living organisms interact with one another and also with the nonliving environment. We will discuss about the ecosystems in more detail at a later stage. However, just to cite an example, a pond is an ecosystem, a river is another ecosystem, and a patch of forest represents a third type of ecosystem. An agricultural field is an example of a man-managed ecosystem. All these ecosystems support certain living organisms which interact among each other and with the non-living components of the environment like water, soil, air, temperature etc.

Biodiversity is not uniformly distributed all over Earth. Certain regions have been endowed with very rich biodiversity while others are not so rich and there are still others which may be considered poor in terms of biodiversity. This happens so on account of various factors like temperature, sunshine, length of days and nights, rain pattern, atmospheric humidity, wind conditions etc. The biodiversity is consistently richer in the tropics and in other localized regions such as the Cape Floristic Province. One of the world's five Mediterranean hotspots. As we approach the polar region fewer species are found there. Floral and faunal diversity depends on climate, altitude, soil type and the presence of other species. On the basis of the richness of biodiversity, certain countries of the world have been assigned the status of Megadiverse Countries. As the name suggests these countries hold higher level of biodiversity as compared to the others. The total number of such countries is sixteen. India is one of them. The others are: Australia, Brazil, Columbia, Democratic Republic of Congo, Ecuador, Indonesia, Madagascar, Mexico, Papua New Guinea, People's Republic of China, Peru, Philippines, South Africa, United States, and Venezuela. India is included in the list on account of the fact that geographically, India occupies only 2.4 percent of the Earth's land area. But the biodiversity present in India accounts for about 7 to 8 percent of the total biodiversity present on the Earth. Obviously India is quite rich in terms of biodiversity. This richness in biodiversity is on account of the richness in terms of habitats and ecosystems. In addition there are twenty five identified hotspots of biodiversity on the Earth. A biodiversity hotspot is a region with a high level of endemic species. These biodiversity hotspots were first identified by Dr. Norman Myers. Most hotspots are located in the tropics and most of them are forests. These areas are rich in overall biodiversity too. In South -Asia, India shares four such hotspots. These are Eastern Himalaya, Indo-Burma, Western Ghats and Sri Lanka, and Sundaland.

Our knowledge about the biodiversity is highly fragmented. Not even 1% of all species that have been described world over have been studied beyond simply noting their existence. It is evident that the vast majority of Earth's biodiversity is in the form of microbes. Also, microbial life is much more diverse than macroscopic life. But most of the attention in this regard is directed towards macroscopic organisms. For example, according to one renowned worker in the field of biodiversity, "On the tree of life….visible life (meaning macroscopic organisms) consists of barely noticeable twigs". Thus most of the biodiversity present on Earth is yet to be discovered, described and understood. The only problem is that time is running out. The Earth is losing species quite fast and we do not have time to describe all or most of the species present on Earth before they are lost. This is the reason why all over the world there is so much emphasis on protection and conservation of biodiversity.

□□□

CHAPTER 3

Classification of Biodiversity

The biodiversity present on Earth is extremely extensive. As explained in the last chapter there is no real estimate of it. Various estimates have been made from time to time and every time new estimates are made the numbers go higher meaning thereby that we are quite far from estimating the actual biodiversity present around us. However, irrespective of the clarity relating to the total picture biodiversity needs to be classified for our convenience. To facilitate the same the biodiversity is identified at three levels: ecosystem level, species level and genetic level. Ecosystem diversity refers to the diversity of Ecosystems and habitats. Even if we look cursorily around us we can easily realize that there are different types of ecosystems or habitats around us. For example, there are ponds, lakes, rivers, grass fields, agricultural fields, forests, mountains, coastal areas, oceans etc. All of these may not be present at the same place or in the same area. But we may find at least few of these.

Now let us first understand what we mean by the term ecosystem. As such the word ecosystem is a contraction of 'ecological system'. It refers to the way nature can be looked at as a system. If we go by the dictionary meaning of ecosystem, it is : "a regularly interacting or interdependent group of items forming a unified whole". In simple terms an ecosystem can be defined as an entity consisting of living organisms and non-living components which can survive on its own using resources available in the environment and energy received from the sun. Hence, for continued survival, an ecosystem must have three functional groups: the producers, consumers and decomposers. By the term producers we mean the green plants. These plants contain chlorophyll. This is the pigment that imparts green colour to the plants. Presence of chlorophyll gives these plants the ability to harness energy coming from sun and to use the same for synthesis of complex chemical molecules which act as food or energy source. First the plants utilize the food or energy for their own survival and growth. Subsequently, the same food is utilized by all other living organisms which do not have chlorophyll and which cannot perform photosynthesis.

At times it may seem so as if certain organisms are not taking food from the plants. For example the carnivores like tiger, leopard, lion etc. or smaller animals like spiders, lizards etc. Reason is that these animals eat other animals. But if we look at those animals which form food for these carnivores, we find that those animals are dependent on plants for food either directly or indirectly. This way plants provide food to the carnivores too although indirectly. Hence, it is essential that every ecosystem must have sufficient number of green plants to convert energy received from sun into food or chemical energy. Only then food or chemical energy will be available to be utilized by various living organisms present in the ecosystem. This is the reason that green plants are called producers. However, an ecosystem cannot be complete if there are only producers. The green plants cannot perform photosynthesis with energy received from the sun in the absence of other resources. The green plants need various other resources from the environment. The simplest ones are carbon, hydrogen and oxygen to form carbohydrate. In reality, the plants use large number of other elements to survive and to perform photosynthesis. Common examples are nitrogen, phosphorus, potassium, sodium, copper, zinc, molybdenum etc. This is the reason that farmers have to go for regular soil testing. Soil testing indicates the status of soil nutrients. Depending on the deficiency the farmers have to apply fertilizers. If they do not follow such procedure, the fertilizers applied are unable to show adequate impact.

Now let us suppose that the producers or green plants are the only organisms in a system, the process of accumulation of food, energy and the nutrients in the body of plants will go on. Finally, a stage may come when the system becomes deficient in one or more of these substances. For continued availability of these elements, it is essential that these remain mobile and also available in the system. This is the reason that for an ecosystem to be complete and successful it is essential that there are organisms which can use the energy and nutrients stored in green plants. These organisms are called herbivores. These are animals which feed upon green plants. So, the energy and the essential elements from plants move into the body of herbivores and a food chain is formed. In an ecosystem the herbivores are called primary consumers as they consume the producers directly. But, only producers and herbivores or primary consumers cannot form a complete ecosystem. The problem of accumulation and locking of energy and essential elements will continue. Some of these will be in the bodies of producers and rest in the primary consumers. In the ecosystem this problem has been solved by inclusion of certain other organisms. The herbivores are eaten by other animals. So, the food chain becomes further extended and the chances of over-accumulation of energy and nutrients are reduced. Animals which eat other animals are called carnivores. Tigers, leopards, cats, certain types of fishes, reptiles, spiders etc. are the common examples. From food chain parlance these animals are called secondary consumers as they consume the primary consumers or herbivores. In certain ecosystems these animals may be the last in the food chain or there may be even other animals which prey upon the secondary consumers. For example the spiders are eaten by certain animals and birds. Lizards are preyed upon by certain other animals. If it is so, these animals which prey upon the secondary consumers are called the tertiary consumers. In summary we can say that an ecosystem must have producers. Without these organisms the ecosystem cannot start functioning. Then there must be different types of consumers for the ecosystem to be stable and successful.

Now we come to another aspect of the ecosystem. The producers and consumers of different types will go on adding dead organic matter into the ecosystem by way of excretion or discarded body parts and carcass on account of death. If the dead organic matter remains intact in the ecosystem, its quantity will grow with time causing problems of space. More serious will be the issue that nutrients and essential elements which are required by living organisms for their survival and growth will go on being locked in the dead organic matter leading to exhaustion of nutrients and other elements from the ecosystem. But, in nature it does not happen so. We find that so many organisms ranging from small to large ones die regularly. Also, the living organisms regularly produce organic waste till the time they are alive. All such organic materials vanish from the environment sooner or later. For example fallen leaves disappear in few days while fallen tree trunks may take months or years to disappear. But nothing remains there permanently. This disappearance takes place as another class of organisms is there in the environment or ecosystem. These organisms are called decomposers. They feed upon dead organic matter to obtain energy for their growth and survival. These organisms include scavengers and decomposers. For example, certain mammals like dogs, hyena etc. and birds like crows and vultures etc. act as scavengers. They feed upon the dead materials and carcass. In the process the energy and nutrients are transferred into the bodies of the scavengers. When these animals and birds produce excretory materials the nutrients and also some energy go back to the environment. On their death the remaining energy and nutrients go back to the environment. Similarly, there are small insects and other animals which feed upon the discarded organic waste and other similar materials. They extract energy and nutrients from there. They too discard part of the nutrients and energy during their lifetime in the form of waste and discards. Finally on their death the remaining energy and nutrients are returned back to the ecosystem. In the process certain portions of the organic materials are decomposed and the rest are converted into finer pieces. Finer pieces are easily attacked by another class of organisms called decomposer organisms.

The decomposer organisms in the ecosystems are mostly bacteria and fungi. As these are very small in size, they perform their task very slowly. For example if a log of wood is decomposed by fungi and bacteria it may take years for these organisms to decompose the log. The decomposition will take place millimeter by millimeter from the outside to the inner core. But if the termites start feeding upon the same log, the log may be decomposed in few weeks. Reason is that the termites digest part of the material themselves. In the process they get energy and nutrition. Rest of the material is broken into fine pieces by the termites. The fine pieces are readily decomposed by bacteria and fungi etc. In fact the alimentary canal of termites has certain types of bacteria living there which help the termites in the digestion of the materials present in wood. Similarly, if soil has earthworms and organic material gets added to the soil, the organic material decomposes quite fast. Reason is that earthworms eat upon the organic matter and extract energy and nutrition from there. The undigested material is defecated by the earthworms in fine form which is easily degraded by bacteria, fungi etc. This is the reason that earthworms are utilized to convert organic waste into compost. The method is called wormi-composting. Also, for the same reason soil which has good population of earthworms is more productive than another soil with same constitution sans earthworms. Long back the famous scientist Charles Darwin had appreciated the usefulness of earthworms and he had written a book on earthworms. The book was entitled "The Formation of Vegetable Mould". He used to call the earthworms as "Greatest Plougher of Fields". The earthworms not only help in decomposition of organic materials, but also create burrows in soil thus bringing soil from deeper layers to the surface and also these organisms create tunnels for aeration of deeper layers of soil. One another group of animals which perform this job is the millipedes. Along with earthworms, they continuously perform their job and help in building soil nutrition. This is the reason that soil which has good population of earthworms, millipedes etc. give better productivity.

Finally, bacteria, fungi etc. decompose the dead organic matter available in the ecosystem into simple compounds and elements. This is how the essential elements and nutrients are brought back into the environment and the cycling of essential elements and nutrients is completed. Result is that these substances become available again to the producers and from the producers to the consumers in the ecosystems. The small animals, fungi and microbes which perform these functions are rarely noticed by casual observer. Here, one is reminded of the non-biodegradable waste like plastic. If we leave pieces of paper, cotton cloth, wood, and plastic on soil, we will find that pieces of paper disappear very soon, a little later the pieces of cotton cloth will disappear. Wood may take some more time to disappear while the plastic may remain there intact for months and years. Reason is that nature has not produced organisms which are efficient enough to decompose plastic. On the other hand, through evolution, nature has produced variety of organisms which can decompose natural products like plant leaves, wood, cotton etc. Paper is also a manufactured material. But it is not synthetic in nature. It is made from natural materials like wood pulp. Hence the same organisms which decompose wood can decompose paper too. This is the basis of composting which yields manure or fertilizer. Organic waste is buried in soil. First insects, earthworms, millipedes break the materials into fine fragments and then the bacteria and fungi decompose the fine fragments into simple molecules. On the other hand plastic and similar other synthetic materials have to be disposed using special methods. Otherwise these materials remain in the environment intact for very long, creating problems.

Ecosystems can be of different types. For example, forest is a particular type of ecosystem, lake or pond is another type of ecosystem, while agricultural areas are the examples of man managed ecosystems. Thus the ecosystem diversity represents different types of ecosystems which are present around us. These ecosystems also exemplify distinct habitats nurturing different types of species. Plants and animals found in a pond or lake are not the same as those living in the forest. Important reason is the difference in environmental conditions in the two ecosystems. Hence, if the ecosystem diversity grows in a geographical area, the environmental conditions for different species of living organisms to survive become more varied. As a result the type of organisms present in the geographical area will become greater and we can find greater number and variety of organisms in the same area.

In a particular ecosystem the number of species plays important role in deciding how the ecosystem will function. A general thumb rule is that more the number of species in an ecosystem, stronger and more stable will be the ecosystem. Reason is that for the same kind of job there will be several species. Even if few of these organisms are unable to function, others may perform. On the other hand if there are only few species for a particular job and due to some reason or the other these species are eliminated, the entire ecosystem may collapse. This explains why monoculture is not advisable in any ecosystem. Presence of mixture of species ensures functioning of the ecosystem under wide scale of conditions. For example if a forest has only one type of trees and there is some disease or infection which may destroy the species, entire forest ecosystem may vanish. Few years back a similar problem had emerged in saal forests in Central India. A particular type of insect was killing the trees in large numbers. There was danger of complete destruction of the forests. Luckily the problem could be tackled successfully before it was too late. Another important feature is that different species doing the same job in an ecosystem are also likely to have complimentary roles. For example, plants which require direct sunlight and those which can grow in shade can produce more biomass per unit area, if they grow together, as compared to when these two types of plants grow separately. In fact the shade plants may not at all grow in the absence of plants which provide shade. Similarly, in any ecosystem certain plants may provide only food to the primary consumers, others may also have chemicals with medicinal or pesticidal properties and still others may contribute by way of controlling soil erosion while a fourth class of plants may play their role in cleaning water bodies or absorbing pollutants from the atmosphere. In the presence of such diversity the ecosystem will function more efficiently. Efficiency of the ecosystem can improve further if there are several types of organisms to perform individual roles. For example, if there are herbaceous plants, shrubs and also trees in an ecosystem to play the role of producers, the ecosystem will be more efficient as compared to another one where there are only herbaceous plants to act as producers. Let us suppose there is fire in the ecosystem. The herbaceous plants will be easily eliminated and the ecosystem may collapse. The same will not be the case with the ecosystem having herbs, shrubs and trees. Even if the herbs disappear the others will survive to keep the ecosystem going. This is the reason that with increasing biodiversity the efficiency of ecosystem goes up.

Species diversity refers to different types of species present in a particular situation. If we talk of one ecosystem, the species diversity of the ecosystem will mean the types of species present there. If we consider a geographical area, the species diversity will mean the types of species of all the organisms present in the area. On the same lines the species diversity of a region or a country would represent the entire array of species in the region or in the country. It would include all the species of microbes, plants and animals present there. As discussed earlier, different types of

A pair of vultures and their nest on a tree. The number of these important scavengers, has reduced drastically in recent years.

Jhum or shifting cultivation a threat to natural forest ecosystems

Several varieties of mango at an exhibition depict biodiversity within one species

Two varieties of wood apple show difference within the same species

ecosystems are likely to have different types of species. For example, a pond may have algae, aquatic angiosperms, aquatic and amphibious animals while a forest will have terrestrial plants and animals. It is possible that few species may be common in both the ecosystems. But, in general, the two ecosystems will support different types of species on account of the prevalent environmental conditions. Even in the same type of ecosystem e.g. forest, the number of species and their population will depend on the environmental conditions of the area where the ecosystem i.e. forest exists. For example, if a pond or forest is situated in a tropical region, the species diversity will be different as compared to a pond or forest located in subtropical region or temperate region. Similarly, altitudinal location of an ecosystem will also influence the species diversity of the ecosystem. For example, a forest at high altitude in the Himalayas will have different species of plants and animals as compared to a forest which is at the foot of the Himalayas. So, species diversity of an ecosystem is governed by various factors and the total of all such diversity constitutes the species diversity of the Earth which will include all the species present on Earth.

Genetic diversity represents the diversity at genetic level within individual species. We need to understand that various individuals belonging to one single species may look similar to each other. But it is not possible that they will have the same genetic composition. This will be so even if the two individuals have the same parent and even if they are twins. There is always some amount of difference in the genetic makeup of individuals. It will be so irrespective of the species they belong to. It is so in case of animals as well as plants and also in case of the microorganisms. At times, the genetic diversity may show itself in the form of difference in physical or morphological features and we may be in a position to detect the difference through superficial examination. We may take the example of any organism. For example all the mango trees are included under one species, Mangifera indica. But all the mango plants are not similar. Some varieties are large trees while others are medium sized while still others do not grow beyond a certain height. The leaf size and shape also differ. The fruits produced by different varieties of mango trees also differ in their appearance and other properties like sugar content, fibre content etc. In the same way two trees belonging to the same variety may look quite similar. Still there will be certain differences between them. These differences are on account of the difference in the genetic makeup of different varieties and different individual plants. Similarly, in case of humans we find different races where the skin colour, body features, body size etc. differ markedly. Even in case of the same race different individuals differ from each other. Such differences are due to the difference in genetic makeup of different races and then in individuals belonging to the same race. Similarly, in case of other organisms too we can find differences between different individuals which signify differences in the genetic makeup. It is likely that quite often differences in morphological or physical characters may not be obvious. Two individuals may look alike. But, their genetic makeup will have differences which can be identified through detailed study of the genetic material.

In most of the living organisms DNA (deoxy-ribose nucleic acid) is the genetic material. Small numbers of organisms have RNA (ribose nuceic acid) as the genetic material. Hence, for all practical purposes we may consider the DNA to be the genetic material which determines the characteristics of the organisms.

It is a general misconception that people with white skin are at advantage. One reason is that they are considered more attractive. But, we must realize that people with darker skin can withstand the adverse effects of solar radiations much more efficiently than those with fair skin. With growing danger of ozone layer depletion, possibility of more UV rays reaching the earth is bound to increase. Dark skinned people can withstand the adverse effects of UV rays much more. Hence, increased UV radiation reaching the Earth will affect the fair skinned people much more readily than those with dark complexion. They may become easy victims of skin cancer and other associated problems caused by the UV rays.

Thus the ozone layer depletion has put the dark skin people at a distinct advantage.

For the readers who are not aware about the working of DNA, let us understand the mechanism how DNA decides the genetic characteristics of an organism. DNA is a double stranded helical structure. It is formed by linking together of large numbers of monomers, which are called nucleotides. In the cell the DNA is present in the chromosomes which are found in the nucleus of the cell. The number of chromosomes present in the nucleus of a particular species is fixed. For example, we humans have 23 pairs of chromosomes in each nucleus. The total DNA present in the chromosomes constitutes the entire genetic material of the organism. The DNA consists of four types of nucleotides and the total number and sequence of nucleotides in the DNA decide the genetic character of the organism. Different organisms have different numbers of chromosomes. Also, the DNA content is different in the chromosomes of different organisms. Thus, total number of nucleotides and the sequence of nucleotides vary from one organism to another. The DNA provides template for the synthesis of a particular type of RNA called messenger RNA (m-RNA). Depending on the sequence of nucleotides in the DNA and the length of the DNA participating in the formation of the m-RNA, the m-RNA is synthesized which has certain length and a particular sequence of nucleotides. In this way the differences in the size and structure of DNA molecules are reflected in the size and structure of the m-RNA molecule. The m-RNA molecule directs the synthesis of protein molecules in the cells. Some of the proteins function as enzymes and drive the chemical reactions in the living organisms. Thus the differences in DNA result in formation of different types of proteins in different organisms which finally decide the enzymatic activities in different organisms. Here we need to understand that DNA strands are very long. But the entire length does not participate in the synthesis of proteins. Only certain segments may participate. The segment of DNA which can decide one character in the living organism is called a gene. So, it can be said that one gene represents a particular sequence of DNA occupying a particular location on the chromosome. That particular sequence of DNA is responsible for the synthesis of a particular type of m-RNA and a particular type of protein which ultimately leads to one particular character in the organism. This is why one gene is considered to be responsible for one character.

Quantity of DNA and the sequence of nucleotides in the DNA vary from one organism to another. As a result the genetic makeup of organisms differs from one another. For example, the genetic characters of humans are different from those of a cow or goat or tiger. Similarly, the genetic character of a teak tree is different from a peepal tree or a saal tree or a deodar tree. As explained in the previous paragraph this difference is caused due to differences in the size and coding of DNA. Every organism has large number of genes and together they decide the total makeup of the organism. For example, people who have the gene for fair complexion, they have fair skin. On the other hand people who have the gene for dark complexion develop more pigments and their skin is dark. Similarly, other genes decide about our body size, hair colour, eye colour etc. If the genes have defects or certain vital gene is missing from the cells, that situation may result in the form of birth defects or hereditary diseases. Thus every individual has a particular set of genes and one species has large numbers of individuals. The variety of genes present in a particular species will be large. Then we have so many species in one ecosystem resulting in further multiplication of the genes. If we take several ecosystems in an area, the numbers of genes present in the area will be much more. Finally, if we consider the entire Earth the total variety of genes or genetic diversity will be too high to be documented. So, we can conclude that the genetic diversity present on Earth is tremendous and it may be very difficult to map all the genes present in different types of organisms.

□□□

CHAPTER 4

Earth and Biodiversity

An important question relating to biodiversity that may come in the mind of anybody is whether the biodiversity on the Earth is constant? A simple answer to the question is a "No". Biodiversity present on the Earth is dynamic at all levels. It keeps on modifying with time. Let us start from the last type as per the classification, i.e. genetic diversity. The genetic compositions of species continue to change on account of natural processes. At times such changes are triggered on account of human interference. In nature genes do change due to environmental factors and also, spontaneously. Such changes are called spontaneous mutation. Now we too have learnt to create changes in the genetic material by applying radiations, chemicals, etc. or by changing the environmental parameters. This is called induced mutation. Such changes in the genetic materials may be reflected in the morphology (external appearance) of the organisms or certain inherent characters may change. For example in domestic animals and crops mutations are induced to result in higher yield, better nutritive content, resistance towards diseases, tolerance for drought etc. Also, it is quite common to observe that farmers select crop varieties which give higher yield or which are disease resistant or drought resistant, depending upon their requirements and the prevalent conditions. There the farmers are indirectly utilizing the changes occurring naturally without human interference. Similarly, a cattle farm manager will give preference to animals which are strong, hardy and more productive. Obviously, the farmers or the farm managers do not get into experiments like induced mutation or selective breeding etc. They generally do selection at the stage of seed collection in crops or at the stage of mating in case of animals. The farmers always look at the best plants in the field and keep their seeds for sowing in the next season. The animal breeder deliberately allows mating of individuals which have superior quality. Subsequently if he has to wean certain individuals from the stock, preference is given to the animals which are stronger, more productive and superior in other ways. Those animals are allowed to continue while those with inferior qualities are sacrificed. If they go on doing so year after year they may achieve substantial improvements in the desired character or characters they like. In this way by selecting certain individuals from a population, we provide those individuals better opportunities to survive and propagate. This process goes on in nature too. For example, individuals in a population which are hardy in character, more resistant to diseases, more efficient in terms of defense or more efficient to adapt to changed environment etc., especially to harsher environment survive better as compared to individuals which are deficient or weak in those characters. In course of time, the superior individuals outnumber or eliminate the deficient individuals or varieties. This is how selection pressure works.

Similar kind of change takes place at species level as well. Their number in any community does not remain constant. It continues to change with time depending on the prevalent conditions. We know that community structure is represented by the variety of species present in an ecosystem combined with the population of individual species. It changes in short term as well as in long term. On the other hand, within a particular community there are regular alterations in the types of species and populations of different species. Such changes are caused on account of ecological and physical factors. At the level of ecosystem too there are similar changes and we can find that the species composition and abundance of different species in a particular ecosystem do not remain constant. Changes in the environmental conditions are reflected in the ecosystem structure. Sometimes it may be easily perceived while at other times it may be obvious only on closer examination. For example, if we take the example of a lake or a forest, changes in the environmental conditions will bring changes in the forest or lake ecosystem. Certain species may disappear while new species may be successful in establishing themselves with change in the environmental conditions. For example, in a forest if there is sufficient greenery and the carnivores are not high in number, the population of herbivores will increase at fast rate. Till a stage it will continue to be so. By that time the carnivores will be at advantage. They can get prey easily and abundantly. Due to better food supply and less completion for food, their numbers will start growing. It may continue like this till the numbers of carnivores become so high that the herbivores are killed in larger numbers than they are produced. Then the herbivores will start decreasing in number. With decrease in numbers of the herbivores, the carnivores will feel the pressure. They will have to work harder to find food and the old and weak ones may not get food at all. Also, due to lack of adequate nutrition reproduction rate will slow down. Hence, the number of carnivores will start decreasing and it will reach to a level when the herbivores and carnivores form a balance. Also, there is possibility that the herbivores may again find opportunity to grow in number at faster rate and the earlier cycle may be repeated.

Also, human interference can change the biodiversity of an ecosystem or an area. For example, introduction of new species in an area may lead to reduction or elimination of the existing species. Introduction of water hyacinth is an example. Water hyacinth is a weed and it grows very fast. Due to its presence natural algae and other plants are eliminated from water bodies. Also, several types of fish are unable to survive in water bodies occupied by water hyacinth. Similarly, in agriculture the age old tradition has been of mixed farming i.e. in the same area or in the same farm different species were cultivated simultaneously. Recently, monoculture i.e. growing of a particular species or variety became more common. Large tracts of land are used to cultivate a single species of crop. Further restriction is brought into play by sowing a single variety or strain of the crop in the entire area. This is now being practiced widely. As a result the other species and varieties are eliminated from the ecosystems. In forestry as well monoculture has become common. For example natural forests have been cleared and teak, eucalyptus or sal plantations have been done on large scale. This kind of activity can eliminate the other species of trees from the forest ecosystems.

A suitable example of total elimination of a large mammal due to human interference is of cheetah. Till almost the middle of 20th century cheetah was present in our country. It preferred grasslands and lived there. The grasslands provided adequate food to the cheetahs by supporting adequate number of herbivores. Also, the cheetahs could easily hunt while hiding in the tall grasses. Then came the time when the grasslands were converted into agricultural fields. On the one hand the natural herbivores started to become rare as these animals were considered threat to the crops. On the other hand it became difficult for the cheetahs to hide themselves. In the absence of natural prey the cheetah was forced to prey upon cattle and other domesticated animals which brought them in direct confrontation with people inhabiting the areas. Even otherwise hunting of cheetahs was a popular sport for the rich. cheetah-human conflicts provided suitable excuse for hunting down the animal. As a result the last cheetahs were killed in 1947. From then onward there are no cheetah in the wild in India. Recently efforts are being made to reintroduce this animal in the wild by bringing them from other countries. However, doubts have been expressed by some of the experts about the success of the initiative. Tiger, rhino, elephant, leopard etc. are dwindling in numbers in the country due to various factors. We will be discussing those factors in later sections of the book. Introducing one more species of large animal may add to the pressure on the ecosystems concerned. Also, the probabilities of human animal conflicts may rise further.

We are aware of the fact that most of the deserts which exist today were not deserts few hundred or few thousand years ago. Most of these areas were healthy forests or farm lands. On account of human interference the forests disappeared and the areas became deserts. In case of farm lands unscientific farming practices converted the productive farm lands into deserts. Obviously, with kind of change the species of plants inhabiting the affected areas had to change. The earlier species mostly disappeared and new species of plants established themselves there. Changes in the species composition of plants triggered changes in animal composition too. With time the same took place and thus the entire ecosystem changed including the species composition and biodiversity present there.

In case of rivers and streams dam construction has often been found to alter the species composition and biodiversity present there. It happens so mainly on account of changes in the flow pattern, creation of reservoirs and submergence of the adjoining areas. In case of ponds and lakes introduction of certain alien species can eliminate either partially or fully the existing species. There are large numbers of examples in this regard where introduction of particular species or varieties of fished resulted in elimination of existing species or varieties. A well known example is of related to Gobindsagar

Lake. Accidental entry of silver carp in the lake has created problems by way of eliminating to a large extent the native catla and mahseer fishes. A recent report from Manipur has highlighted the fact that at least 15 local varieties of fish are endangered on account of introduction of exotic varieties which are considered 'high yielding'. The list of fish varieties which are endangered includes nganap, sareng, khoibi, ngasep and ngamu. Two species of weed plant Lantana camara and Parthenium (Carrot grass) have established themselves in large areas in the country. Both of these got introduced in the country by mistake. Both of these are hardy. They proliferate very fast and eliminate the native species of plants in forests and in farmlands resulting in changes in biodivesrsity of the affected areas. There are many more examples of similar nature. We may deal with few of them in later sections.

□□□

CHAPTER 5

Present Status of Biodiversity on Earth

By now we can easily appreciate that the Earth is quite rich in terms of biodiversity. We can easily observe the richness of biodiversity if we move from one place to another or we shift from one type of ecosystem to another. We find that quite different types of organisms are encountered at different places. For example if we start climbing a mountain, we find broad leaf trees and associated shrubs, herbs etc. at the bottom. As we go up we find that the broad leaf species become less common and other types of trees start appearing. These are generally gymnosperms like Pinus, Cedrus etc. with needle like leaves. Also, the associated shrubs and herbs change as we climb up. Finally after a certain altitude trees do not exist. That level is called the tree line. Beyond that only smaller plants exist. These plants may be very different from what was seen at the base of the mountain or at intermediate heights. Thus due to change in altitude the plant biodiversity keeps on changing. Parallel to that the animal biodiversity too changes. For example the animals that are found at the bottom of the mountain range disappear at higher altitudes and different types of animals exist there.

If we move from one geographical area to another the biodiversity keeps on changing and we encounter new types of plants, animals and microorganisms. This is the reason that the total biodiversity on Earth shows huge numbers. There have been various estimates of the total biodiversity present on Earth. But we do not have any clear idea about how many species exist on earth. Estimates range from 5 million to 100 million. The United Nations Environment Programme (UNEP) has estimated that there may be about 13 to 14 million species of living organisms existing on Earth. Certain other estimates suggest that there could be between five to fifty million species on Earth. But, the tragedy is that so far only about 1.75 million species have been identified or described. It clearly means that a very large portion of the organisms are not yet identified and if we take into account the complete description of the organisms, the number is much less. This is the reason that we are informed regularly about the discovery of new species of organisms. On an average between 5 and 10,000 new species are discovered each year. Most of them are insects. Another important issue is that many new species are discovered but these are not yet classified. Rough estimates suggest that nearly 90% of all arthropods are yet to be classified. Most of the terrestrial diversity is present in the tropical forests. For example, Brazil's Atlantic Forest which is considered a hotspot of biodiversity is estimated to contain roughly 20,000 plant species, 1350

Two tigers in wild. These and other carnivores are important for survival of natural forests.Poaching and loss of habitat have threatened their very existence.

Moss plants on rocks. These small plants can survive in adverse conditions and help start ecosystems in barren areas.

Mangrove area being sacrificed for agriculture. Mangrove ecosystems are unique as they play an important role in protecting the coastal areas.

Dead corals, following the flow of municipal sewage, found close to an island in Andaman. Coral areas support very large varieties of organisms.

vertebrates, and millions of insects. About half of these occur nowhere else in the world.

At this point it is important to note that these new discoveries are not related to only tiny organisms. Larger organisms are also discovered regularly. For example, few years back Fillipino and UK wildlife researchers discovered a new species of flightless bird on the tiny forest island of Calayan in northern Philippines. The Hindustan Times, reported the discovery in its issue dated 18th August 2004. The bird was dubbed as Calayan rail. There is a joint venture by scientists from more than 70 nations which is carrying on a 10-year project to complete the first census of marine life. Midway to their programme they have informed that they found 78 new species of fish. The same included a 3-metre rocket shaped jelly fish called Physconect siphonophore. It was a unique discovery. They also found tiny sponges in the south Atlantic which were carnivorous. During their 538 expeditions, Census of Marine Life explorers collected hundreds of thousands of specimens. On the basis of these specimens it has been concluded that more than one thousand of them were new to science. These species have been given their Latin names (scientific names). Many more specimens are awaiting description. It is likely that from among them more new species will be identified. Concurrently, Census database experts have helped in creating Internet Frameworks to integrate information from the work of all marine biologists to make global assessments. Through these assessments it is estimated that newly discovered and described marine species, since the year 2000, may now exceed 5,000. Among these there are more than 150 marine fishes. During the census microbiologists found millions of unicellular marine organisms, it is expected that a large number of them may be new to science.

As noted above discovery of new species of organisms is quite common. An important factor is the improvement in techniques related to collection of specimens, their preservation and their study and comparison with global database. Also, more and more scientists are devoting time and effort towards study of biodiversity world over. This is happening as large numbers of nations and international organizations are providing funds and other facilities for those studies on account of the better understanding of the value of global biodiversity. For example, a new species of freshwater stingray was discovered in Thailand in a river in 2004. The stingray has been given the name Himantura kittipongi in honour of the fish expert who had discovered the new species. In another survey done in the seas off Indonesia, scientists found 24 new species of fish including two types of shark. Also, twenty new species of coral and eight shrimps, which were not known in past, were discovered. In 2005 a new species of carnivore was discovered in the Kayan Mentarang National Park, Borneo, Indonesia. The animal looks like a cross between a cat and a fox. In Tanzania on the Mount Rungwe a new species of African monkey was discovered in 2005. The monkey (Lophocebus kipunji) is brown in colour, about three feet long with an erect crest of hair on its head.

In India too new species have been discovered regularly. Also, plants and birds which were considered to be extinct have been rediscovered. For example, a medicinal plant Begonia tessaricarpa which was considered to be extinct was discovered in Arunachal Pradesh after more than a century in 2006. A bird called Large Billed Reed Warbler, which was considered to be extinct, was seen after 140 years near Kolkata in 2007. Quite important was the discovery of a new species of monkey in Arunachal Pradesh in 2004. The monkey was named Macaca munzala or Arunachal macaque. The monkey is very shy. On being suspicious of human presence in the vicinity, it quickly disappears in the forest through the undergrowth. Probably, that was the reason that so far it was never described. In this regard it is important that it is the first new macaque species discovered during last about hundred years. A new type of frog called Pignose Frog was recently discovered in the Western Ghats. A new type of ant Discothyrea sringerensis has been found in Karnataka. This ant behaves as if it is dead when it encounters any dangerous situation. Indian egg-eater snake which was considered to be extinct has been spotted again quite recently. Also, from Assam two species of frog, new to science, were discovered. Similarly, scientists investigating Ovale malaria, a form of the disease thought to be caused by a single species of parasite. However, scientists have found that the parasite is actually two different species which are similar.

Thus it is obvious that our knowledge about the biodiversity present on the Earth is far from complete. We know only about a small fraction of the organisms present on Earth. The rest are yet to be discovered and described. Another important issue about the spread of biodiversity is that only about seven percent of the world's land area supports about fifty percent of the biodiversity present on Earth. Hence, if this small portion of the Earth's surface suffers devastation and the living organisms are exterminated either completely or partially from these biodiversity rich areas, the Earth will be losing large portion of its biodiversity. The devastation may be due to natural reasons or it may be man-made. As far as natural devastation is concerned, not much can be done about it. However, effort must be made to exclude the possibility manmade devastation. If it cannot be eliminated completely, efforts should be made to reduce it. To achieve the same we have to understand the ways in which we can cause devastations which may lead to erosion in biodiversity. The next step will be to take positive action to eliminate or at least reduce such activities. If we consider region wise, the tropics show maximum biodiversity on the Earth. It is presumed that the tropical region may be supporting about five million species of living organisms. When this is the situation at species level, the magnitude of genetic diversity will be beyond imagination. For example, a unicellular (consisting of only one cell) organism may have few hundreds of genes. Larger organisms have many more genes. If we take into consideration the estimated number of organisms present in the tropical region the number of genes present in them will go into billions and if we calculate the number of genes on the entire Earth it would be unimaginable. On the ecosystem level too, the diversity is quite large as variety of ecosystems exist on the Earth. Even similar ecosystems existing in different environmental conditions may not have the same organisms. For example, lakes in warmer climates will have different types of organisms as compared to the lakes in cold or alpine region. It is quite likely that there may be some commonality. But the differences will be clearly evident. Similarly, forests in tropical region will have different flora and fauna as compared to forests in subtropical or alpine region. This is so because the types of organisms present in a particular ecosystem depend on various environmental factors such as the climate, rain fall, soil conditions, quantity and quality of water present etc. Similar ecosystems present in different regions will differ in all or at least many of such factors.

If we lose a particular ecosystem in any part of the Earth, it is quite likely that along with the ecosystem, we may lose certain species which are specific to that particular ecosystem. In areas where endemism is prevalent the impact of losing a particular species or a group of species will be even more serious. Obviously, this kind of loss will result in loss in overall biodiversity.

At this point one important fact to be kept in mind is that all the species which existed on Earth at some point of time are not present today. Earth is estimated to be in existence for the last about four billion years. Very recently it has been calculated by scientists at the Cambridge University that the solar system was born about 4.567 billion years ago and Earth reached its current size around 4.467 billion years ago. Earlier it was thought that the formation of Earth i.e. the clumping of gas, dust, and other materials to form Earth required only 30 million years. The new study claims that the process could have taken up to 100 million years. However, important is the fact that life was not there since the beginning of Earth. Life started much later. Scientists are of the view that life has been certainly present on Earth for about 600 million years. This estimation is based on the discovery of fossil remains of animals. The earliest fossils discovered so far are about 600 million years old. But that does not mean that there was no life before that. It is quite likely that life existed even before 600 million years. But, there are no fossil records for the earlier period. One important reason could be that the life forms which existed before 600 million years ago were simpler and not suitable to be converted into fossils. In any case irrespective of the time when life started on Earth it has not been a smooth journey. Scientists have found evidences to indicate that mass extinctions have been taking place at different times leading to disappearance of almost entire or most of the life on earth present at the time. Five such mass extinctions have been identified by scientists so far. There is possibility that evidences for more of such extinctions may be discovered in future. The first mass extinction is estimated to have taken place around 450 million years ago. The other ones were around 350, 275, 195 and 65 million years before now. It is estimated that the extinction which took place around 275 million years ago was the most devastating. Around 95 percent of species present at the time was lost. The latest extinction which took place about 65 million years ago is well known and quite often discussed. Reason is that the dinosaurs disappeared from Earth on account of it. Generally it is believed that disappearance of dinosaurs was on account one cataclysmic event. However in 2010 British researchers have claimed that dinosaurs disappeared on account of a sudden fall in sea temperature by about 9°C. The fall in temperature started about 137 million years ago and that was the first step towards their extinction. This controversy apart, it is important for us to understand that all those mass extinctions were on account of natural reasons.

Human race had nothing to do with the mass extinctions which took place earlier. But, those mass extinctions should serve as warning for the human race. An important lesson is that once a species is extinct, it is gone forever. There is no possibility that the dinosaurs will ever reappear on Earth. Hence human race must be careful and it must not force living organisms towards extinction. Once they are gone, they will never come back. If we look at the recent extinctions, it becomes evident that human factor was the main culprit. Reason is obvious. During the last few centuries or so human race has become very ambitious and it wants to control all the processes on Earth an even in the outer space. There are several well known examples of complete extinction of species due to human activity. Dodo is one of them. Dodo inhabited the island of Mauritius and it had so much freedom that it slowly lost its ability to fly as it did not find it useful. At the beginning of the 16th century the Portuguese were the first inhabit the island. Then they started hunting the bird for food. At the same time they introduced various animals to the island which killed the birds or destroyed their eggs. Within 100 years Dodo became rare and the last bird was killed in 1681. Another example is of the Tasmanian tiger. It was the largest marsupial which was carnivorous. The animal had disappeared from Australia about 2000 years ago. But it was widely found in Tasmania. The problem started with large scale sheep farming in Tasmania in the late 19th century. As the sheep were killed by the tiger, it was declared a pest and reward was given for killing the animal. As a result the animal became fast extinct. As per available records, the last animal died in 1936 in Hobart zoo. Another very well known example is of the Passenger pigeon. During the beginning of 19th century the bird was present in huge numbers in Northern America. There have been descriptions stating that the flocks were at times so large that the sunlight was completely obliterated and days appeared as dark as nights. Large scale hunting resulted in its complete extinction within one century. In 1914 only one bird was alive. It was named Martha. That one surviving specimen died in Cincinnati zoo in 1914. Another interesting example is of Golden toad. It was seen till about twenty years ago. The number decreased drastically in 1987. Till 1989 few individuals were spotted. Since then the species has not been spotted indicating its total extinction. As per (IUCN) International Union for Conservation of Nature compilation more than 840 species of animals and plants have become extinct during the last 500 years. In the year 2006 large numbers of species were formally classified as rare or endangered or threatened. Scientists have estimated that there are millions more species actually endangered which have not yet been formally recognized. About 40 percent of the 40,177 species assessed using the IUCN Red List criteria, are now listed as threatened species. These 16,119 species may become extinct any time.

The United Nations has been concerned about the threat to biodiversity and the pressures which lead to extinction of species. In the process it constantly brings out reports to highlight the issue. A report published in 2006 warned that the current extinction rate is about thousand times to the normal rate of extinction which has been there before human factor started playing its role. The report further highlighted that about 25% of all the mammals were on the verge of extinction. Birds were more endangered. Fifty percent of them were in the list of threatened ones. In 2008 the Red List was released on 6 October 2008, at the IUCN World Conservation Congress in Barcelona. According to the list, almost 25% of mammals (at least 1,141 of the 5,487) were at risk of disappearing forever. For about 840 species the data were not sufficient to draw any conclusion. Many of them could be expected to be threatened.

In nature along with extinction a parallel process goes on. That process leads to evolution of new species resulting in appearance of new types of living organisms on Earth. This has been happening since the time life came into existence. It is logical to conclude that the process of evolution continued after the episodes of mass extinctions. As a result new species evolved and deficiencies caused by the extinctions were compensated and the Earth's biodiversity was restored. This is the reason that even after so many mass extinctions the biodiversity on Earth continues to remain rich. But it is important to understand that the process of evolution did not bring back the lost species. Evolution could result in appearances of new species. That is why we do not find evidence of reappearance of extinct species. Another feature of evolution of new species is that the process has always been very slow. Hence, it must have happened in due course of time. Also, there is evidence to prove that with time the maze of life on the Earth underwent continuous expansion. The process of evolution brought more complex organisms into existence. Result was that with passage of time more complex organisms were added to the existing array of life on Earth. But, the new and complex species did not replace the earlier organisms. They were added to the existing spectrum as nature has always favoured evolution and addition of greater number of species of living organisms on Earth. That is why the process of evolution has continuously resulted in expansion of diversity. Another parallel development has been that with passage of time interaction between living organisms became more complex. To successfully carry on such complex interactions new players have been introduced in the form of new organisms. For example, when we travel from a moist forest to some dry forest we find that the tree species, associated animals, birds and even insects do not remain same. They change and if we try to introduce the plants and animals from one type of forest to another there is no guarantee that the effort will succeed on account of the different environmental requirements of the plants and animals.

Similarly, when we pass from region of high rainfall to low rain fall, we find that the flora and fauna undergo obvious changes. For example, in our own country if we travel from Kanyakumari in south to Kashmir in the north or from the Himalayan region towards the desert in Rajasthan, we will find that the flora and fauna goes on changing continuously. This kind of change is necessary because a particular species of plant or animal is adapted to certain specific environmental conditions. For example, the camel cannot survive in moist or cold weather. Among fruit trees mango, jackfruit, wood apple, palm etc. cannot grow in cold climate while apple, peach, apricot etc. will not grow in the warm climate. This is the reason that if the conditions prevalent at a site undergo change, the existing species disappear and they may be replaced by other species which are suited to live in the new environment. In ecological term this phenomenon is called Species Turnover. There is another parallel phenomenon which results in more variety of organisms. This is called Geographical Turnover. Geographical turnover is exemplified by organisms which are similar otherwise but constitute different species on account of geographical separation. A suitable example is the macaque monkey. In Brahmaputra valley we find Assamese macaque, in north of Godavari we can find Rhesus macaque while south of Godavari we find the Bonnet macaque. All these are the progeny of one single species. These emerged as distinct species on account of geographical separation. Island habitats commonly provide examples of this type of turnover. For example, in Andaman and Nicobar and Lakshadweep we find several species of birds and other animals which are restricted to these areas. These organisms are given the status of distinct species by the scientists on account of geographical isolation. Birds or animals which are quite similar to them can be found at other places on the mainland. But, they are not classified or bunched together to make one single species.

□□□

CHAPTER 6

Threats to Biodiversity

Earlier, we learnt about mass extinctions which exterminated large number of species from Earth. Every time after a mass extinction new species evolved and took the place of those which were extinct. As a result Earth's biodiversity went on restoring itself and also spreading. We also understand that human race had no role to play in those historic extinctions. But, recently, a new phenomenon is being noticed. The extinction rate is faster than the rate at which new species are evolving and this kind of extinction is more prominent in areas like tropics where the ecosystems are richer in terms of biodiversity and also the ecosystems are much more fragile. Nature has not to be blamed for this kind of extinction. It is the human race which is responsible for it. This is why it is often said that man is creating conditions which may lead to the next cycle of mass extinction. Another tragedy with this type of extinction is that there is very little possibility that life may regain its earlier richness. Important reason is that we are destroying species selectively. A special phrase has been coined by the scientists to describe mass scale disappearance of species. The phrase is "Empty forest syndrome". This refers to the export of Asian animals in millions for use in pet shops, pharmacies, restaurants etc. Estimates suggest that during the past decade more than 35 million animals were exported in legal way from Asia. It is estimated that illegally hundreds of millions more could have gone out. As a result the biodiversity had to suffer. The phrase "Empty forest syndrome" refers to the same as there are areas in forests where no big animals are left. The animals so taken legally or illegally end up as pets in Europe and Japan. Traditional medicine trade of China is another reason for the demand of several varieties of animals in large numbers. For example, about 16 million sea horses were traded during the period and bulk of it was in dry form. Obviously, it was for use in medicines. It has been observed that China is the prime destination for this kind of wild life. There the animals are used in medicines. The recent disappearance of large number of tigers from India is also alleged to be connected to China. Bone and other body parts of tiger are in great demand there for use in traditional medicines. The skin is purchased by people in Europe and various other countries as trophy or for decoration purpose.

Convention on International Trade in Endangered Spices (CITES), experts looked into the records relating to imports and exports numbering 53000 for the period 1998 to 2007. It was found that 35 million animals were exported during the period, of which about 30 million were from the wild. The animals commonly exported were pangolins, tortoise, butterflies, leopard cats, birds of different types, exotic fishes, macaques, reptiles etc. Illegal smuggling of animals and plants is rampant all over the world. Experts are of the view that volume of illegal smuggling is many times more than legal trade. Large numbers of reports regularly appear in the media relating to detection of different animals on airports. Efforts are made to carry the animals in illegal manner from one country to another. Even live snakes, cubs etc. have been detected on airports. The persons involved try to conceal the animals in their luggage etc. At this point an important fact has to be considered. Illegal trade brings more pressure on the biodiversity as the traders are always in a hurry to transport the merchandize to the destination. Also, they have to conceal the materials during transit which brings additional pressure on the survival of the traded organisms. It is estimated that 60 to 80% of the animals traded illegally never reach their destination alive. They die during transit.

Destruction of forest is an important factor in causing threat to the biodiversity. For example, half of the primate species present today are threatened to become extinct on account of destruction of the tropical forests and associated poaching and illegal trade. Scientists have found that presently there are 25 species of primates which are highly endangered. Eleven of them are found in Southeast Asia, six in Africa, five in Madagascar, and three in South America. In all there are 634 species of primates presently living in different parts of the world. 48% of these are classified as threatened species as per IUCN (International Union for Conservation of Nature). Few of the most threatened are Cross river gorillas, Golden headed langur, Eastern black crested gibbons, Northern sportive lemurs. Among all these Cross River gorillas are the most endangered African apes. The threat is on account of poaching and habitat destruction. Climate change caused by excessive emission of greenhouse gases is posing an additional threat to biodiversity. A recent IUCN report has identified 10 species which are extremely vulnerable on account of climate change. These species are: arctic foxes, clownfish, koalas, emperor penguins, Leatherback turtles, staghorn corals, ringed seals, quiver trees, salmon, beluga whales. Obviously, growing content of greenhouse gases in the atmosphere and consequent impact on climate change, this vulnerability is going to increase. So far there is no indication that greenhouse gases in the atmosphere are going to reduce or stabilize in near future. As we are aware separate negotiations are going on the subject under the aegis of the United Nations. If those negotiations succeed, the impact on climate change may be reduced or nullified.

On account of these factors an assessment carried out three or four years back indicated that about 25% of all the mammals present on the Earth are facing the danger of imminent extinction. In case of birds the danger is even bigger. About 50% of all the species of birds present on Earth were found to be facing risks of extinction. Habitat destruction was the main factor leading to the threat. It is not difficult to visualize the threat. About 15 million acres of primary forests are being cleared every year from the face of the Earth. About one third of the mangrove areas have been lost in a short span of last about twenty years. Similarly, other types of habitats are also facing degradation and disruption.

It is estimated that about 800 species of organisms including trees, mammals, birds, reptiles, amphibians are found in habitats which are being disrupted on account of human developmental activities. If these regions are disrupted further, chances are that these species will disappear. In case of our own country there are several examples of confinement of various species in single regions. Asiatic lion is confined to a small region in Gujarat. Kashmir stag or Hangul is confined to a very small area in Jammu and Kashmir. Sangai or Manipur Brow-antlered deer is confined to a wetland in Manipur. Gangetic dolphin is restricted to a small stretch of river Ganga. Nilgiri tahr is another well know n example which is restricted to a small area in the Nilgiris. Himalayan Musk deer, four-horned antelope and one-horned rhino are other well known examples of species which are restricted to small regions. If those areas are further disturbed, chances of their survival will reduce further. Aquatic habitats have also been disturbed all over the world on account of human interference, pollution, dumping of wastes, over-fishing etc. resulting in threat to the organisms present there. Even very large oceans are not free from such threats. For example, during the span of last half century appreciable decline has been recorded in the population of more than 65% of large fishes in the North Atlantic. For other areas authentic data are lacking. But it is not expected that the situation is very different. However, the aquatic ecosystems which are facing maximum threat are those which are in the freshwater.

At times wrong scientific decisions have put organisms under threat. A very pertinent example is related to the sparrows. In The Great Leap Forward implemented in China, a countrywide programme was launched to finish four common 'pests'. Those were sparrows, rats, flies and mosquitoes. As far as the last three are concerned those were certainly pests. But sparrows were included in the list on account of wrong scientific understanding. The entire country started working overtime to get rid of all the four 'pests'. Nests were destroyed in millions. During the night millions of people used to disperse to the countryside and make continuous noise so that the sparrows could not alight. The alarmed birds had to keep on flying till they fell to their deaths. Millions and millions of the birds were thus killed. Also, various other bird species might have become victims of that folly. It is unthinkable that sparrows could be targeted alone. It was good that later findings brought to light the fact that sparrows were quite important in controlling the insect pests attacking crops. Minor damage which those birds caused to crops was of no consequence. Finally, the sparrows were spared and these birds were allowed to live peacefully. But during the intervening period how much damage was done to the bird fauna of the country has never been estimated.

In our own country due to our mistakes large number of animals and plants have entered the threatened category. For example, several varieties of fish are on the verge of extinction. An important reason is the disappearance of aquatic bodies. For example in Manipur during the early 20th century there were around 100 large lakes. At present only three survive. The others are dead. Obviously, the habitat has shrunk drastically. Another reason for the disappearance of the local varieties of fish is the introduction of high yielding varieties which have eliminated the local varieties. A third factor is the pollution of rivers on account of dumping of sewage and solid wastes and contamination due to pesticides and fertilizers received with agricultural runoff. In Orissa the indigenous fish varieties are under threat on account of uncontrolled fishing, mining and various other developmental activities. During last about seven to eight years in case of Chilika Lake alone the fish species have come down from 261 to 154 as per the information provided by the Chilika Development Authority. Similarly, in the Hirakud reservoir the number of fish species has come down from more than 180 to 43 during the past 20 years. Kerala is an important fish producing state of the country. More than 250 species of fresh water fish are found there. In recent years it was observed that the fish production in inland water bodies had come down drastically to about one third. The main factors were pollution, reclamation of aquatic bodies and introduction of exotic varieties.

We know that certain species of animals regularly migrate from one area to another. To undertake migration the animals need safe corridors. Asian elephant is a classic example. Important reason is that the Asian elephant once roamed in a vast area which ranged across southern Asia right from the Tigris-Euphrates basin (now in Iraq). It was found across the Indian subcontinent and extended into Indo-China. Various islands in the southeast also supported elephant populations. In the northward direction the elephant population could be found up to the Yangtze River and even further. At present the Asian elephant has a vastly reduced range. Another problem is that the habitat is fragmented. Thus the animal is forced to live in isolated groups. At present there are more than hundred fragmented populations in the entire range. For example, in Sumatra Island alone there are more than 40 isolated populations. India has more or less similar number of isolated populations scattered in the four regions. We know that for long term survival every species needs viable populations with adequate habitats. Elephant groups need several hundred square km at minimum in the short term and several thousand square km for long term viability. Extending the elephant areas beyond a certain limit is quite difficult on account of pressure on land. An alternative is to maintain corridors between different habitats which are otherwise isolated. Such corridors permit the animals to move from one area to another. This kind of migration helps the animals in one area to mingle with the animals of other areas. In India alone a total of 88 corridors have been identified which are currently in use by the elephants. Twelve of the corridors are in North-western India, 20 in Central India, 14 in Northern West Bengal, 22 in North-eastern India and 20 in Southern India. Estimates made by scientists working with elephants brought out the fact that more than 77% of the corridors are in regular use by the animals. But with passage of time the corridors are getting eroded and human interference is constantly increasing in the corridors. This situation leads to human elephant conflicts and forces the animals to get confined to isolated habitats. This situation is never conducive for the survival of the animals. Recently, a tragedy killed seven elephants while they were migrating. A railway track has been laid across their migration route. The elephants were crossing the track when a speeding goods train hit the group killing seven elephants. It became a news item as large animals were involved and seven of them were killed. Everyday large numbers of smaller animals, birds etc. are killed while crossing roads, highways, train tracks. But hardly people notice them.

Medicinal plants have proved extremely useful to the entire humanity. In early stage of evolution the entire human population was almost totally dependent on medicinal plants for its survival against various kinds of diseases and ailments. More important is the fact that even in this modern age the medicinal plants are used in big way as such or for manufacture of medicines or for preparing various formulations. Certainly, there are large numbers of drugs and medicines used in modern treatments, which are not obtained from plants. These are synthesized in laboratories and factories from chemicals. But many of these are such that their discoveries were made on account of information obtained from plants. The general impression carried by people that modern system of medicine is dependent on synthetic chemicals alone is not correct. In fact it owes a large number of products to plants, either directly or indirectly.

We know that the western system of medicine owes a lot to the Greek physician Hippocrates. He propounded the theory that diseases were due to natural factors. He used large number of herbal medicines to treat his patients. Roman philosopher Dioscorides, who had great influence on the modern system of medicine, in his 'De Materia Medica', collected information about more than 600 types of plants with medicinal properties.

Let us take the case of a very common drug, aspirin. It has antipyretic, analgesic and anti-inflammatory properties. But more importantly aspirin is recommended as a protective drug against strokes and heart attacks. It provides protection against recurrence of stroke or heart attack. For people beyond 40 years of age it reduces the chances of first attack by more than 40%. Aspirin is also effective in triggering the immune systems against bacteria and viruses. It also helps in delaying the symptoms of cataract in persons of old age. In fact large numbers of experts are of the view that success of aspirin has caused hindrance to medical research. Doctors and researchers are not searching for better options as they have aspirin.

Around 400 B.C., Greeks and Romans had discovered that bark of the willow tree (Cortex salicis) carried antipyretic and analgesic properties. Its decoction was administered as medicine during that period. During 18th century willow bark tea was a common remedy for chills and fever in England. By the early part of 19th Century the active principle, 'salicin', present in the bark was identified. It was a glucoside of salicylic acid. On chemical degradation, salicin yielded salicylic acid, which was more effective as analgesic, anti-rheumatic and antipyretic. In 1859 a German Chemist, Hermann Kolbe succeeded in laboratory synthesis of salicylic acid. However, the synthetic chemical caused gastric irritation. Viable solution was found in 1898 in the form of acetyl derivative of salicyclic acid, which was less irritating to the gastric system and also more palatable. From then onwards the chemical is being used as aspirin.

Malaria is a big killer in India and in several other Asian and African countries. However, we may not be aware that till few centuries back malaria was a scourge for Europe. Greeks discovered that people living near marshes and swamps suffered more. Italians considered that it was caused by bad air from marshes and hence the name, 'mal aria' (meaning foul air) was given. In 17th Century it was discovered that the bark of the Peruvian Cinchona tree could cure malaria. Till the 17th century powdered bark of Cinchona tree was the only treatment for malaria. In 1820, the active principle 'quinine' was isolated and since then it has been used for treatment of malaria. During the 19th century plantations of Cinchona trees were established in India and Java by the British and Dutch to extract quinine on large scale. The initiative helped Europe to get rid of malaria.

The history of the pain killer morphine is even more interesting. Since around 9th century, Opium poppy (Papaver somniferum) was used to treat pain and also to anaesthetize patients. The active principle, morphine, was first isolated in 1806. In 1826, E. Merck of Germany produced an analgesic drug based on morphine and even today various formulations containing morphine are in use to provide relief from severe pain.

Use of Rauwolfia serpentina (Sarpagandha) has been known to Indian Ayurveda practitioners for more than 4000 years. Its root was used to cure insect bites, snake bites and mental illness. Reserpine was the first active principle isolated from this plant and it has been regularly prescribed for schizophrenia. Now it is also prescribed for hypertension and to control high blood pressure.

Another common example is the plant, Aloe vera. For thousands of years the leaf of Aloe has been used to treat skin problems, burns, sunburns, rashes, wounds etc. Succulent leaf of the plant has soft tissue and mucilage. The tissue and the mucilage are highly soothing and inhibit growth of bacteria and fungi. This is the reason that today large numbers of skin creams, sun protection creams, shampoos etc. contain extract from this plant.

Similar is the case of Digitalis purpurea (Foxglove). The plant has been used from early times for treatment of heart diseases. Foxglove leaf contains a number of glycosides. Glycosides increase the activity of all forms of muscles, specifically those of the heart and arterioles, resulting in stronger heartbeats. Digitalis also causes irregular pulse to become regular and it improves the nutrition of the heart by increasing the amount of blood reaching the heart. Action of the drug on kidneys is of equal importance. In small or moderate doses, it is a powerful diuretic and a valuable remedy in dropsy, especially when this is connected with problems of the heart. It has also been employed in the treatment of internal hemorrhage, inflammatory diseases, delirium tremens, epilepsy, acute mania and various other diseases.

If we look at a much recent example, taxol, we find that it is the most promising anti-tumour agent. In the 1960's the National Cancer Institute of USA collected plant specimens from all over the world to screen for anti-cancer drugs. Bark of the Pacific Yew tree (Taxus brevifolia) was also screened and taxol could be identified as a potent anticancer drug. However, the problem was that the trees had to be sacrificed to produce the chemical. Later it was found that needles (leaves) of the English Yew (Taxus baccata) contained a chemical which could be converted to taxol chemically. Presently, taxol is prepared from the leaves and it is commonly being used for treatment of ovarian cancer and breast cancer.

Almost similar is the case of vinblastine and vincristine. These are two alkaloids, found in the leaves of commonly grown garden plant, periwinkle (Catharanthus roseus). These two chemicals as well as vindesine and vinorelbine which are semi-synthetic derivatives of vinblastine, inhibit division of living cells and hence these are being considered future potent drugs to cure cancer.

Few years back, Dr. B.S. Blumberg, Nobel Laureate from USA, who had discovered Hepatitis 'B' virus, was in India. Here he got information about the commonly found plant, Phyllanthus amarus (Bhui amla). He could establish that Bhui amla could cure Hepatitis 'B' infection and he obtained two patents on the plant.

It is estimated that in India alone there are 15000 types of plants which have medicinal properties. A large number of these are in regular use in various traditional systems of medicines like Ayurveda, Unani, Siddha, Tibetan system etc. WHO estimates that about 80% of the population living in poor countries directly or indirectly depends on medicinal plants for their day to day health problems. On account of expanding demand the threat in case of medicinal plants is obvious. Important reason is that the dominant source of these plants is natural forests. Even today about 90 to 95% of the medicinal plants are obtained from wild. But the practices adopted for collection of the medicinal plants are generally unsustainable. That brings severe pressure on the habitats resulting in damage to the resource base. Exact quantification of the damage so caused is not possible as reliable information relating to harvest of the medicinal plants form the wild is not available. However a study relating to twenty species of medicinal plants commonly harvested in the country provided information about the approximate number of plants required to be harvested annually to meet the market demand. This study is an indicative of the prevalent situation. The information is given below:

Species	*Approximate number of plants needed to meet the demand*
Asparagus racemosus	70,000
Bacopa monnieri	90,000
Baliospermum montanum	6,500
Coscinium fenestratum	500 (about 30 year old climbers)
Hemidesmus indicus	152,000
Holostemma ada-kodien	46,300
Nervilia aragoana	30,000
Plumbago indica	120,000
Rotula aquatica	7,200
Rubia cordifolia	14,000

This situation existed sometime back. At present the situation may be even worse as the demand for medicinal plants is continuously growing on account of higher demand in the domestic as well as export markets. It is obvious that this kind of extraction will bring undue pressure on the resource and its continuation for years may result in total depletion of the resource base. Similar kind of situation may be there in case of other resource bases associated with biodiversity. That is probably the reason that experiences of the past few decades have clearly brought out that with growing industrialization and economic development, the ecosystems and the biodiversity present in the ecosystems get destroyed or threatened. Large numbers of similar other examples can be readily cited where such threats exist and the same can easily be visualized all over the world and also in our own country. For example, we have already lost large tracts of forests all over the country. Estimates suggest that at the beginning of the 20th century about forty percent of the geographical area of the country was under the cover of high quality forest. The present figures indicate that only about twenty one percent of the country's geographical area is under forest cover. Out of this, only about twelve percent is healthy forest. Rest is either degraded forest or wasteland. This situation has been reached because we always underestimated the value of forests and diversion of forest land was permitted extensively resulting in utilization of forest land for other purposes. With decrease in forest cover the pressure on the remaining forest areas increased on account of increasing demand for timber, wood, forage, medicinal plants, fruits and other minor products obtained from there. As a result, the remaining areas have been regularly overexploited resulting in their degradation. Similarly, large numbers of wetlands have been destroyed and the land so recovered is being used for entirely different purposes resulting in loss of flora and fauna which were suited to survive in aquatic environment. Grasslands all over the country have been shrinking on account of their conversion into agricultural land. Grasslands close to townships and cities have generally been encroached for habitation. The situation with mangroves is not at all different. Mangrove areas have been diverted to agriculture, urbanization, industrialization etc. Peter H. Raven of Missouri Botanical Garden says:

"Plants provide, directly or indirectly, all of our food, most of our medicine, a large proportion of the chemical substances that we use, material for shelter, and fibre for clothing. They protect the top soil, insure the quality of the water that we drink, determine local climates, and ultimately provide food and shelter for all other living beings too. They are beautiful and diverse, and nourish our souls as well as our bodies. Yet we are destroying them at a frightening rate, so that as many as 100,000 of the estimated total 300,000 species may be gone or on the way to extinction by the middle of the 21st century. If we do not take action now, by the end of the century we may have destroyed two-thirds of the plant species we currently use and enjoy.

I emphasize once more that the survival of biodiversity throughout the world depends on the degree to which we approach the ideal of sustainable development around the world. This is a world in which human beings have wasted 25 per cent of the top soil and 20 per cent of their agricultural lands, cut a third of their forests, and changed the characteristics of the atmosphere significantly; one in which we are ending the century as 6 billion

people, consuming or wasting an estimated 45 per cent of the available fresh water. That is not the world that allows much space for the survival of plants or other organisms. Indeed, it is one in which species have been and will be increasingly hounded to extinction."

Source: The Botanica, Vol. 50, 2000

Such diversions have been carried on without taking into account the important role the mangroves play in keeping the environment healthy and in stabilisation and protection of the shorelines against erosion and cyclones. From economical point as well these areas are important as they provide fuel wood, fodder, tannins, fish, hides, wax, honey and various types of chemicals and medicines. These areas also provide suitable breeding environment to various types of aquatic animals. From biodiversity point of view, the mangroves are extremely important as these areas nurture special kind of flora and fauna. Many of these cannot survive once the mangroves are removed or devastated beyond certain limit.

In fact, we can draw a general conclusion for all the natural ecosystems except the deserts that these are regularly shrinking. Only the desert ecosystems have been showing the signs of expansion in the country. It is happening at the cost of the other ecosystems, natural or man-managed. It is a scientific fact that nature does play a role in expansion of the desert ecosystems. For example, change in climate can lead to desertification. Also, prolonged drought in an area can trigger desertification. However, more import is the fact that human activities prove to be catalysts in the process of desertification. We create situations favourable for expansion of deserts. For example, we create conditions which enhance soil erosion leading to desertification. We allow overgrazing by domestic animals which is another important factor in desertification. Creation of soil salinity too helps in land degradation leading to desertification. The same takes place on account of over-irrigation, water logging etc. Unscientific agriculture can also trigger the process of desertification. It is important to understand that desertification happens only at the cost of productive ecosystems. A suitable example is the Aravalli region. Aravalli mountain range has historically worked as an effective barrier against the possible advancement of the Thar desert. On the other side of the mountain range is the fertile plain, which act as the granary for the nation. After Independence, during the middle part of the 20th century, the Aravalli hill system suffered heavily on account of large scale deforestation. As a result the capability of the mountain range to contain the Thar desert was eroded and the desert started advancing. It was apprehended that in due course of time the desert sand could convert the fertile plains on the other side into desert. Luckily, the problem was diagnosed early and corrective measures were initiated. Aravalli Project was started. The aim of the project was to green the Aravalli range and educate people living in the area about the adverse impacts of deforestation. Fuel wood extraction was a major source of deforestation in the area. Fuel wood was used as household fuel and also for making charcoal sale. People living the area were provided alternative avenues to fuel wood harvest. Also, it was found that income of the general population in the area was quite low. Very large numbers of families were dependent on goat rearing which brought heavy pressure on the vegetation in the area. Avenues for income generation from sources other than goat rearing and charcoal making were created and people of the area were encouraged to adopt the same as both these activities prevalent in the region were found to be extremely detrimental to the forest ecosystem. Simultaneously, large scale tree plantations were done to bring back the greenery in the area. An important aspect was that women involved in a big way in the implementation of the project, as they were the direct sufferers on account of degradation of the ecosystems in the area. They had to work harder and spend more time to collect fuel wood and forage on account of vanishing green cover. Also, they had to walk for miles to get water for daily use. Collection of fuel and water is usually the responsibility of women in the rural areas. With degradation of the environment, water availability was also severely affected. During last about three decades or so the Aravalli Project has achieved good success in Haryana and Gujarat. Green cover is spreading and people in the area are now a happier lot on account of better lifestyle and better availability of resources.

Another internationally known example of degradation of fertile land into desert is from the present day Iraq. History tells us that the area between the two rivers, Tigris and Euphrates used to be extremely fertile. It gave birth to the world dominating civilizations of Babylon and Sumer. But now, the complete stretch is a desert and it did not happen on account of natural reasons. Human activities, which were unfriendly to environment, were responsible. Intensive agriculture, animal farming at large scale and extraction of natural resources beyond the limit of sustenance were some of the important factors. As a result the area became desert and the rich civilizations were wiped out. One can cite many other examples where mismanagement on the part of human race has resulted in conversion of highly productive ecosystems into deserts and wastelands. In our country itself there are vast stretches of wastelands in different parts. Historically, these areas were not wastelands. They have turned into wastelands on account excessive exploitation, deforestation, soil erosion, nutrient loss, salinization etc. The next step after wasteland is only desert. If corrective measures are not adopted in time the wastelands can easily turn into deserts.

Causes of desertification:

1. Unscientific agricultural practices such as intensive cropping, excessive application of fertilizers, pesticides, irrigation etc.
2. Practicing shifting cultivation with short cycle.
3. Conversion of forest land for non-forestry purposes.
4. Excessive extraction of ground water.
5. Recurrent drought, failure of monsoon and changes in earth's climate.

Obviously, this total scenario is resulting in great deal of threat to the rich bio-diversity of the country. With every passing year more and more species of plants, animals and other organisms are finding their place in the list of endangered or threatened species. But, we need not get disheartened. This is a universal phenomenon. Most of us have the illusion that developed world is very conscious about the environment, especially

City of Shimla expanding at the cost of natural forest

Natural forest shrinking in Western Ghats due to expansion of agriculture and tree plantation

Asiatic lion now found only in Gir forest in Gujarat

Conventional varieties of seeds on display. Most of these are now disappearing due to lack of cultivation.

Lichens on tree trunk. Air pollution has resulted in their disappearance

An elephant herd in the Western Ghats, highly endangered due to poaching and fragmentation of habitats

about the biodiversity. The fact is not so. Ted Turner, founder of CNN (TV channel), says: "Traditionally, the avenue for attaining wealth has been plundering natural resources, and the history of the United States of America is a telling example. We have chopped down 93 percent of our old growth forests, ploughed under 98 percent of our native prairies, and filled in more than 50 percent of our wetlands." More or less similar is the situation with other developed nations. This is the reason that predictions are being made that up to two thirds of all the species present on this earth are likely to be exterminated by the end of this century. If this forecast comes true, a large number of plants and animals all over the world which comprise the unique natural heritage of communities and countries will disappear. Their place will be taken by opportunistic and globally adaptable creatures such as cockroaches, rats, pigeons, weeds of different types and so on. These species have the capability to readily adapt to disturbed environmental conditions. Also, these opportunistic species can easily eliminate the species which are native to the areas. We have already discussed about Water hyacinth, Lantana, Carrot grass (Parthenium) etc. These weed species are eliminating the native species and degrading the ecosystems.

In last few decades concern about vanishing species of plants and animals has been increasing. It has happened so on account of the realization that several species of plants and animals which were around are no more. Certainly, large animals and plants of economic value have contributed significantly in this regard. Their disappearances have been detected easily as compared to very small animals or insignificant plants. Now IUCN has compiled the Red Data Book which runs into several volumes. It lists over 40,000 species of animals and plants which are under threat to extinction. Again, we need to understand that extinction is a natural phenomenon. It has been going on since life originated on this earth. Large numbers of species of plants and animals which existed in past became extinct. Simultaneously, new species evolved. However, the point of concern is that the present estimates indicate that the world is losing species at rates reaching up to 10,000 times the natural rate of extinction. This rate is alarming as it is estimated to be more than what resulted in the extinction of dinosaurs about 65 million years ago. According to the 'Global Biodiversity Assessment' the extinction of species since the year 1600 has been going on at 50 to 100 times the average natural estimated rate. This rate has increased fast in recent past. It is expected to rise to between 1000 to 10000 time the natural rate in near future. It is not difficult to realize that this kind of development will prove to be catastrophic. We very well know that a species once extinct cannot be brought back otherwise birds like Dodo or Passenger pigeons could have been there with us. At this point let us look at five examples of animals which are considered the rarest. These are:

1. Amur leopard: This species is found in the range which extends from Korea to North-East China and Far East Russia. Only 35 individuals of this species are known to be there in wild.
2. Northern white rhinoceros: Only eight individuals of this species exist and these are in captivity.

3. North Pacific right whale: Less than 50 are present in the range stretching between East coast of Russia to the West coast of Alaska and Canada.
4. Pinta island tortoise: This tortoise originated from the Island of Pinta of the Galapagos Islands. Only one individual, estimated to be between 80 and 100 years of age, named Lonesome George, survives. Several attempts to breed George with similar tortoise varieties have not proved successful. Eggs were produced but the eggs were not viable. Old age of George could be the factor.
5. South China tiger: It is estimated that less than twenty members of this species survive presently in the forests of South China.

   Obviously, the danger is imminent. These species may disappear any time.

There are several species of animals which are endemic to India. If these are under threat in India, it would mean that these are globally threatened. There are many more species which under severe threat. One example which has been in limelight recently is the Indian White-rumped vulture. This bird which was seen in plenty till one or two decades ago has suddenly become rare. This bird plays important role in keeping the environment clean by scavenging upon carcass of animals. A lot of controversy was there regarding the reason behind disappearance of the bird. Finally, it has been realized that the main factor has been the use of veterinary drug Dicofenac. This drug is rampantly misused by people who manage the domestic animals. On account of overuse, the chemical accumulates in the body of animals. When they die and the carcass is left for scavenging, the vultures feed upon them. The chemical is thus transferred to the birds and accumulates in the birds' body and results in kidney failure leading to their death. The other well known example is of the Great Indian Bustard. This bird is found in a restricted area in Gujarat and Rajasthan. During the last few decades number of this bird has been falling fast on account of habitat destruction, associated with occasional hunting. A very well known example is of the Indian Cheetah. Indian Cheetah became extinct in the middle of the last century. The animal's habitat i.e. grasslands were devastated and converted to agricultural areas resulting in their exposure to easy sighting. Simultaneously, the animal was killed in large numbers by the British and the Indian rulers leading to its total extinction in 1947. We are aware about the Asiatic lion which used to roam from Greece to India till about few centuries back. It is now restricted to a small area in Gujarat. That too could be possible because the Nawaab of Junagarh provided protection to the animal after receiving a communication from a common citizen. A bird called Jerdon's courser is another example of forced extinction. It is estimated that very limited number of the bird is surviving in a particular area in Andhra Pradesh. The pressure is on account of destruction of its habitat by developmental activities. Now Himalayan quail is totally extinct. Its habitat was in the foothills of the western Himalayas. It was last seen in 1876. Since then there have been occasional reports of its sighting but without confirmation. Pink headed duck is another example. It was found in Northeast India and Myanmar. Now it is considered extinct as after 1935 there is report confirmed report of its sighting. The last duck was killed in north Bihar. Asiatic two horned rhino which was found from Assam and Bangladesh to Borneo, including Cambodia and Myanmar is not found any more in India and Bangladesh.

Illegal poaching and habitat destruction were the main reasons for its extermination from these areas.

At this point it would be pertinent to discuss a news item which appeared recently in a leading newspaper. The news item refers to the increased poaching of leopards in the country. We know that during the last few years there has been extra focus on the dwindling number of tigers in the country. Government machinery has been condemned by one and all for their laxity to provide protection to the tiger population in the country. The matter was taken up seriously at the highest level and various corrective measures were initiated. Obviously, the poachers have been under pressure. The recent report says that the poachers are now concentrating on leopards in lieu of the tigers. Evidence comes from the fact that during the first three months of 2010 more than 70 leopards were killed in different parts of the country. During 2009 as many as 290 leopards were killed in the country. These were the reported/estimated cases. Wildlife enthusiasts are of the view that many more leopards are killed every year in the country. Their estimate is that about 500 animals are killed annually. Reason is that leopard body parts are suitable substitutes for tiger body parts. Also, leopard skin fetches good price. It is claimed that in international market it may sell for Rs. one lakh per piece. Also, there have been instances of poisoning of leopards by farmers, especially in Maharashtra. Important reason is that with reducing forest areas the leopards stray into human habitations and attack cattle, goats, dogs and even humans. In retaliation people kill them. They surround the stray animals and kill them or they kill them by putting poison in water bodies regularly visited by leopards. Wildlife experts are of the view that if corrective measures are not adopted, very soon leopards will have to face similar situation as being currently faced by the tigers in the country.

In conclusion we can discuss about the numerous threats which the biodiversity on Earth faces. We can also realize that we ourselves are responsible for most of them. IUCN has provided some information in this regard.

It says:

- Habitat loss and degradation affects 86% of all threatened birds, 86% of the threatened mammals assessed and 88% of the threatened amphibians.
- Introduction of invasive alien species that establish and spread outside their normal distribution. Some of the most threatening invasive species include cats and rats, green crabs, zebra mussels, the African tulip tree and the brown tree snake. Introductions of alien species can happen deliberately or unintentionally, for example, by organisms "hitch-hiking" in containers, ships, cars or soil.
- Over-exploitation of natural resources. Resource extraction, hunting, and fishing for food, pets, and medicine.
- Pollution and diseases. For example, excessive fertilizer use leads to excessive levels of nutrients in soil and water.
- Human-induced climate change. For example, climate change is altering migratory species patterns, and increasing coral bleaching.

In this regard it is important to note that we are losing biodiversity at an alarming pace. Estimates suggest that since 2000, 6 million hectares of primary forest have been lost every year. Corals have declined world over. Estimates made in the Caribbean region bring out the fact that hard coral cover in the region has declined from 50% to 100% in the last three decades. 35% of world mangroves have been lost during last two decades alone.

Climate change can also affect the biodiversity as these two are closely related. We have discussed this aspect separately. At this point there is need to emphasize that we need to make additional efforts to minimize the negative influence of various factors listed by IUCN above. By doing so we can ensure that ecosystems are not easily vulnerable to the possible threats posed by climate change. The resilience so generated will help the biodiversity to face various other challenges too.

At this point we need to consider Invasive Alien Species (IAS) as well. It has been concluded by scientists that among the important threats to the native plants and animals and also their habitats the IAS may be considered at the second place only after habitat loss. These are plants and animals which on reaching outside their natural habitats pose threat to biodiversity. In this regard it is important to note that only a small percentage of organisms reaching new habitats and environment become invasive. However, this small percentage may result in great deal of damage to biodiversity and consequently to human health, plants, animals, food security and also economic parameters. In India we find a number of examples of IAS. Parthenium (Carrot grass) is a well known example as a weed. This weed also causes respiratory problems and allergy to people. Lantana is another example. This bushy weed has spread in large areas in the country, especially in the forests and is causing havoc. Water hyacinth is an example of aquatic weed which got introduced in the country. It has spread to almost entire length and breadth of the country and it is interfering on a large scale with normal use of water bodies. Fishing, irrigation, navigation, water sports are being affected in big way due to this weed. Also, its presence in water bodies helps the mosquitoes by providing them suitable habitat and breeding ground. Several types of invasive organisms causing diseases are affecting agriculture in the country. Notable among them are banana bunchy top virus, potato wart, turnip stripe virus, coffee berry borer etc. At other places we have discussed about species of fish, shrimp etc. which were introduced deliberately or accidently in water bodies and in course of time they have turned into menace.

□□□

CHAPTER 7

Status of Biodiversity in India

It is obvious that Earth's biodiversity is not uniformly distributed. Certain regions are richer than others in respect of biodiversity. This difference is due to geographical location of the region and the environmental conditions prevalent there. As we have already seen sixteen nations have been classified as 'Megadiverse Countries of the World'. This nomenclature is because these countries support exceptionally rich biodiversity. India is one of these mega-biodiversity nations as it also supports very high level of biodiversity. If we look at the geographical location of India the reasons become obvious. India is located between latitudes 6° and 38° N and longitude 69° and 97° E. It is situated in the tropical belt. It is surrounded by the Himalayas in the north, in the east is the Bay of Bengal, on the western side is the Arabian Sea and in the south the land mass ends at the Indian Ocean. This geographical situation results in an unusually long coastline extending to about 7500 kms and also there is great deal of variation from one area to another in the parameters which determine the environmental conditions. Rainfall is one such parameter. The Western Ghats receive about 2000 mm rain while certain areas of Rajasthan, Gujarat and Ladakh receive only about 100 mm of rain on annual basis. Similarly, the average annual temperature varies extensively from one area to another. Solar energy received per unit area is not the same at different locations. It differs appreciably from one region of the country to another. Also, India occupies quite large area. It has a land mass of about 330 million hectare. On account of these factors a wide spectrum of habitats exists in different parts of the country. For example, certain areas have tropical rainforests while other areas support alpine type of vegetation. Still other areas are known for the temperate forests present there and at the other extreme are the coastal ecosystems. If we travel from one part of the country to another we can easily experience the variations in the climatic conditions, environment, flora and fauna etc. For example, certain areas are covered by thick forests while others are occupied by grasslands, or wetlands. Still other areas are occupied by harsh deserts. The coastal belt has totally different environment and associated biodiversity.

Physically, India can be divided into four well defined regions: the Himalayan Mountains, the Gangetic plains, the Deccan plateau and the island groups, namely Andaman & Nicobar and Lakshadweep. The highest peak in the Himalayas in India is Kanchenjunga at 8586 m. There are various other mountains and hills which are not as high. But, even these are high when we compare them with the other mountain ranges of the world. Towards the south of the main Himalayan massif lies the Lesser Himalayas which has peaks going up to more than 4500 m. If we move further south, there are the Shivaliks where the peaks are up to about 1500 m. The northern plains extend from Punjab to Assam. These plains extend in south into Gujarat and end with the Rann of Kachchh. A number of major rivers like Ganga, Yamuna, Brahmaputra, Ghaghra etc. pass through this region. As far as the climatic condition is concerned, the Indian climate is dominated by the Asiatic monsoon. The rains are brought from the south-west during June and October while dry winds are received from the north during December and February. The period between March and May is generally dry and hot.

India also figures prominently in the biodiversity hotspots of the world. In all twenty five hotspots of such have been identified at global level. Out of these eight have been recognized as the most important ones and two of these extend into India. One is Western Ghats/Sri Lanka and the second one is the Indo-Burma region which includes the Eastern Himalayas. Apart from these two hotspots, India has 16 major forest types, 42 vegetation types, 10 bio-geographical zones and 26 endemic centers. In addition, India has two major realms, the Palaearctic and Indo-Malayan and three biomes: the tropical humid forests, the tropical dry deciduous forests and the warm deserts and semi-deserts. From bio-geographical point of view India has been divided in ten distinct regions. These are:

Trans Himalaya	Deccan Peninsula
Himalaya	Gangetic Plain
Deserts	North-East
Semi-Arid	Islands and
Western Ghats	Coasts

Obviously, these regions are different from each other in many ways. The environmental conditions in one region are not same as in the other. On account of the same these regions support different types of flora and fauna resulting in variations in the biodiversity in. Cumulative effect of these factors is that with only about 2.4 percent of land mass (about 330 million hectare), India accounts for about 7 to 8 percent of the total biodiversity present on Earth. For example, more than 160 species of crops and 300 species of wild relatives of cultivated crops are believed to have originated in India. With respect to forest cover, India does not have the ideal situation i.e. 33 percent of the geographical area under forest cover. However, the forests present in India are quite rich in terms of variety. These can be classified into sixteen major groups and 221 types ranging from the evergreen tropical rain forests in the North-East, the Western Ghats and Andaman and Nicobar Islands to the dry alpine scrub forests in the high Himalayas. Between these extremes there are semi-evergreen rain forests, deciduous monsoon forests, thorn forests, subtropical pine forests and temperate montane forests. This kind of variation in forests obviously results in floral and faunal diversity. Large varieties of plants and animals find suitable habitats to flourish in these forests.

Grasslands: Another important vegetation type in India is the grasslands. The grasslands are called steppes, savannas, prairies and pampas in different parts of the world. The geographical area under grasslands in the country is about four percent or about 12 million ha. Indian grasslands can be classified into five distinct types. These are Sehima-Dicanthium type found in peninsular India; Phragmites-Saccharum-Imperata type found in the alluvial plains of Ganga and in the deltaic region of West Bengal; Themeda-Arundinella type found in the mountains and hill regions; Dicanthium-Cenchrus-Lasiarus type found in north western part of India and Temperate-Alpine type present at high altitudes in the mountains. The grasslands are rich in biodiversity. These grasslands support about 250 genera and more than 1250 species of different classes of organisms.

Wetlands: Wetlands spread all over the country provide another distinct class of habitat. Broadly speaking, wetlands are shallow water bodies in which water keeps up for most part of the year. During the dry season water recedes below the surface level. The biotic community changes with time. It changes from aquatic/marshy to mesophytic type. Wetlands are considered complex hydrological and biogeochemical systems and these are recognized as distinct ecosystems falling between the aquatic ecosystems and the terrestrial ecosystems. In our country, wetlands are situated in different geographical areas starting from the Himalayas to the Deccan plateau. Obviously, the climatic conditions are different in different regions and there is large scale variation in topography in different regions. As a result the wetlands show different characteristics in different regions. The wetlands also differ in their origin, nutrient status, thermal characteristics and the vegetation they support. Taking these into account the wetlands are classified into different types such as Glaciatic wetlands, Tectonic wetlands, Oxbow wetlands, Lagoons, Crater wetlands, Saltwater wetlands, Urban wetlands, Man-made wetlands, Reservoirs, Mangroves, Coral reefs, Creeks etc.

Space Application Centre used remote sensing technique for the identification of inland and coastal wetlands. In the process 27,403 wetlands were identified covering 7.6 million ha area. The diversity of organisms present in any wetland depends upon the size of the wetland, its geographical location and the climate of the area where the wetland is situated. Wetlands in India are rich in floral and faunal diversity. For example, there are about thirty species of plants found in wetlands which are under rare or threatened category. Similarly, there are twenty six species of animals found in the wetlands which are endangered. Common examples are sangai, dugong, fishing cat, gangetic dolphin, Estuarine crocodile etc. This is the reason that twenty five wetlands of India have been recognized to be of International significance under the Ramsar Convention. Total area of these wetlands is more than 677000 ha. This international convention was formulated in 1971 in the city of Ramsar (Iran) with the exclusive aim to provide recognition to the wetlands all over the world so that these habitats may be protected. Under this convention the signatory nations take steps to protect and conserve the wetlands. Especial emphasis is laid on the wetlands which are recognized to be of international significance. Indian wetlands recognized under Ramsar Convention are-

Ashtamudi, Sasthamkotta and Vembanad-Kole in Kerala; Bhitarkanika and Chilika in Orissa; Bhoj Wetland in M.P.; Deepar Beel in Assam; East Kolkata Wetlands in West Bengal; Harike Lake, Kanjli and Ropar in Punjab; Keoldeo National Park and Sambhar Lake in Rajasthan; Kolleru Lake in A.P.; Loktak in Manipur; Point Calimere in Tamil Nadu; Pong Dam Lake, Renuka Wetland and Chandertal Wetland in Himachal Pradesh; Hokera Wetland, Surinsar-Mansar Lakes, Tsomoriri and Wular Lake in J & K., Rudrasagar Lake in Tripura, Upper Ganga River (Brijghat to Narora Stretch) Accordingly, efforts are being made to provide intensive protection to these wetlands on priority basis. Also, efforts are on to protect other wetlands of the country. Ninety four wetlands have been included in the National Wetland Conservation & Management Programme of the Government of India which is implemented by the Ministry of Environment and Forests. Total area of these wetlands is more than 3 million ha. Now it is well understood that wetlands play an important role by way of various kinds of substantive benefits. Few of these are: flood control, recharge of aquifers, decontamination and cleaning of sewage, protection of shoreline. In addition the wetlands act as suitable habitat for aquatic flora and fauna. Many of the wetlands act as habitats during the winter season for migratory birds. A number of wetlands are important tourist destinations providing recreational avenues and also income to the local people and others associated with tourism industry. Wetlands in general are an important source of fishes all over the world. It is estimated that at globally about one billion people depend on fishes of different types for use as food and important source of protein. Maldives consumes maximum quantity of fishes as a country. Next is Iceland and then in descending order are Kiribati, Japan, Seychelles, Portugal, Norway, Malaysia, French Polynesia and South Korea. Although India does not come in the list, in certain regions of the country fish is an important component of daily diet. Also, India earns substantially through export of fish and fish products. Globally, about 35 million people are estimated to be associated directly with fishing and aquaculture. The stake of developing countries is much more in this regard as 95% of the work force comes from the developing countries.

Deserts: Deserts in India cover about two percent of the land area and these can be easily classified into three categories: sandy Thar desert, salt desert of Kutch and cold deserts of high altitude in the states of J & K and Himachal Pradesh. The three types of deserts have their distinct flora and fauna further adding to the country's biodiversity.

So far about 90,000 species of animals and more than 49,000 species of plants have been identified and described by the Zoological Survey of India (ZSI) and Botanical Survey of India (BSI). The details are available in table 2 and table 3. But, this is not the complete picture. Large number of animals and plants are yet to be identified and described. Hence, it is expected that the total biodiversity value of India will grow with time as more areas are explored and intensity of exploration improves all over the country. Another important characteristic of Indian biodiversity is that India has a high ratio of endemic species. About 33 percent of Indian plants are endemic i.e. they are found naturally only in India and nowhere else. These endemic species are mostly

Different types of corals and sea shells, on sale at a beach in Alexandria, Egypt. Marine biodiversity is endangered due to these activities.

Birds in cage for sale as pets. Captivity endangers their life.

Brahma Kamal, now very rare due to overexploitation

Pitcher plant - an insectivorous species, rarely seen now

found in Western Ghats, North-East, North-West Himalayas and Andaman and Nicobar group of islands. Similarly, more than 60 percent of the amphibian species are endemic. In case of lizards too about 50 percent of the species are endemic. High degree of endemism is prevalent in other groups of organisms too.

Marine and Coastal Ecosystems:

Much of the biodiversity present globally is found in marine and coastal habitats. These habitats include tidal flats, coral reefs to ocean floors with soft sediments which do not receive any light. In these habitats new species are being discovered regularly. Still the number of species present in the marine systems is less than those present on land. The deep sea bottoms which were earlier considered to be generally barren are now considered to be the habitat for very large number of small invertebrate animals. Main reason is that new species in large numbers are being discovered from middle depths of different oceans and seas. Similarly, very small animals, which are not easily visible without microscope, may be present in thousands in few grams of sand from coastal area or sea bottom. These minute animals play very important role in the sustenance of marine ecosystems. If we look at the faunal diversity of marine ecosystems of India we find that twenty phyla out of the total 32 are present there. In all about 12,400 species of animals have been recorded so far. As far as coastal zone is considered India has a very long coastline extending to about 8000 km. Hence, the coastal ecosystems deserve to be considered separately as they form a distinct type of habitat and support rich biodiversity. In this regard it is important that the coastal zone, which represents only 18% of the Earth's surface, accommodates about 60% of total human population. Around 70% of the world's cities with population of more than 1.6 million are located in the coastal zone. In 1995, over 2.2 billion people lived within 100 km of coasts. This accounts for 39 percent of the world's population. In 1990 the figure was only 2 billion indicating 10 percent rise from 1990 to 1995, i.e. in only half decade. There are various factors responsible for this kind of concentration in coastal regions. One of these factors being the direct connection with other parts of the world through sea route. Traditionally, sea route has been used for international trade and travel. Another factor is that the coastal areas are the meeting points for different rivers with the seas and oceans. Such meetings result in formation of estuaries, deltas, marsh lands etc. Mixing of fresh water with sea produces conditions which are suitable for distinct type of flora and fauna. On account of the presence of these, the productivity of the coastal zone is higher than the open sea and also most parts of the land. This is the reason that about 90% of world's total fish catch is obtained from the coastal zone. This is also evident from the fact that the aquatic habitat of the coastal zone is only about 8% of that of the world oceans. But this zone is responsible for about 18 to 33% of total primary production. Tourism brings additional revenue in the coastal areas and also provides avenues for work to the people living in the area. Also, greater contribution of coastal areas to tourism, trade and international transport have resulted in greater degree of development of the coastal areas in general. Hence, people from other areas migrate and settle in coastal areas.

Although in Indian context a little more than 60% of the fish production comes from the coastal capture fisheries, it contributes to the economy of the country in a big way. Also, other resources present in the coastal areas contribute to the economy of the country and the people living in the coastal areas.

Biogeochemically also, the coastal zone is more important as it acts as receiver for 80-90% of organic matter and serves as a sink for an estimated 50% of the global carbonate depositions. Carbonates are formed due to absorption of carbon dioxide from the atmosphere and its reaction with calcium. This kind of deposition is responsible for maintaining the carbon balance in the atmosphere. Corals play significant role in this deposition. This is the reason that globally, there is more concern about conservation of the coastal zone. With decrease in productivity, the absorption of carbon dioxide from the atmosphere will go down which will result in larger buildup of carbon dioxide in the atmosphere. We very well know that carbon dioxide build up in the atmosphere will lead to Green House Effect causing global warming. We are already experiencing some impact of global warming. If the warming becomes more intense, the effects will be catastrophic.

In Indian context too the coastal ecosystems play vital role on account of the resources available there such as highly productive habitats and rich biodiversity. On account of the Indian land mass being surrounded on three sides by seas and there being two groups of islands on the two sides of the mainland the total coastline is about 8000 km. The mainland accounts for 5,853 km. Andaman and Nicobar Islands and Lakshadweep group of islands account for about 2094 km. The coastal belt is home to about 25% of the total population of the country. They live within 50 km from the coasts. On account of the land shape, the mainland coast is divided into two parts: West Coast and East Coast. The West Coast is in contact with the Arabian Sea while the East Coast is adjacent to the Bay of Bengal. In addition to these two coasts there are three island groups. Lakshadweep group of islands is situated in the South Arabian Sea wile Andaman and Nicobar Islands are in Bay of Bengal. The West Coast is generally exposed with heavy surf and rocky shores and headlands. On the other hand, the East Coast is shelving with beaches, deltas and marshes. The East Coast is also relatively low-lying with extensive alluvial plains and deltas. The Indian coastal zone is endowed with a wide range of ecosystems such as estuaries, lagoons, mangroves, backwaters, marshes, rock coasts, sandy stretches, coral reefs and offshore islands. The aerial extent of some coastal marine ecosystems in India is given in **Table-1.**

Corals: The coastal ecosystems in India support unique flora and fauna. Among these the coral reefs form the most dynamic ecosystem providing shelter and nourishment to thousands of marine plants and animals. They protect the coastlines against erosion by tides and cyclones as these living structures or their dead remnants from protective shields against the onslaught of normal waves and also against stronger waves during cyclones, tsunami etc. Corals form three major types of reefs, namely atoll, fringing and barrier. Indian subcontinent which consists of more than 8000 km of coastline and subtropical climate has only few areas with corals. Other areas in the world with similar conditions support much more coral formations. In India the reefs are present along the east and west coasts in a limited way. The total area of coral reefs in the country is estimated to be more than 2270 sq. km. However, we find all the three types of reefs in the country. Fringing reefs are present in the Gulf of Mannar and Palk Bay. Platform reefs are present along Gulf of Kutch in the Northwest. This area has some of the most northerly reefs in the world. Patchy reefs are present near Ratnagiri and Malvan coasts. The Andaman and Nicobar islands have fringing and barrier reefs. A very long barrier reef (more than 300 km long) is also there on the Andaman and Nicobar islands. Lakshadweep group of islands have extensive coral reefs which are mostly atolls except one which is of platform type.

From evolutionary point of view, corals are very primitive animals and they are made of simple tubes with just one opening. But, these corals can build enormous colonies with the help of their skeletons, which contain lot of calcium. These colonies can form even islands. Examples are Lakshadweep, Mauritius, Barbados etc. Also, the Great Barrier Reef of Australia has been built by corals.

The coral ecosystem is most productive because it can retain and recycle nutrient elements within the ecosystem as well as within animal-plant associations. It is evident from the fact that among various ecosystems in the sea, reefs support the highest number of species. The total number of reef species on the Earth is not known. However, it is estimated that a single reef in South East Asia may have up to 3000 species while a reef in the Caribbean region may have about 1,000 species. Only tropical rainforests have more number of species than the coral reefs. Also, it is an established fact that the reefs contain many more major animal groups (phyla) than any other ecosystem on land or in the sea. In India about 200 different species of corals have been recorded. In addition, sponges, mollusks, crustaceans, echinoderms, fishes, reptiles, mammals, fishes are there associated with the coral reefs in India. Total number of these species exceeds 1400.

Corals in the country are facing different types of threats. Most of it is anthropogenic. Some natural threats are also there like waves and storms. But these threats cause only occasional damages. Also, during the months of October and November there are cyclones which are associated with strong wind. High speed wind causes strong waves which damage and break the corals. Also, sand and other materials are deposited on the corals resulting in damage to them. Heavy rain on land and in coastal areas can damage the corals by way of inflow of large quantities of fresh water into the sea, especially in bays which are partially enclosed or in lagoons. Entry of large quantities of fresh water reduces the salinity of water and deposits large quantities of nutrients and sediments in the coastal area. All these are harmful to coral growth and survival. As far as anthropogenic reasons which cause damage to corals are concerned, these include sedimentation, surface runoffs containing pollutants, excess nutrients, discharge of household sewage in coastal water, thermal pollution on account of addition of hot water from industries into coastal areas, unscientific and destructive fishing practices etc. Addition of nutrients in the sea through anthropogenic activities has indirect impact as well. The nutrients encourage growth of phytoplanktons which in turn provide support to the larvae of starfish. Certain starfish are coral eating. They destroy coral population. This is the reason that destruction of coral eating starfish is an important strategy in the management of coral areas. The starfish are captured and buried under sand where they die.

Mangroves: Mangroves form a particular type of unique forest ecosystems in the coastal zones close to the river mouths in the tropical and subtropical regions. The vegetation is dominated by special type of plant community which is capable of tolerating high concentration of salt. The vegetation is adapted to periodical inundation alternatively by salt rich water of the sea and fresh water from the land. These plants can easily survive the tidal pressures without being easily damaged. In fact this property of the mangrove vegetation protects the coastal areas against tidal onslaughts in the tropical and subtropical regions of the world where these plants survive at the interface between land and sea. There they form salt-tolerant forest ecosystems especially near river mouths in the areas which are inundated during high tide and exposed during low tide.

In our country mangroves can be found along the two coasts and Andaman and Nicobar Islands. On the east coast mangroves can be found in the Gangetic delta of Sunderbans, Mahanadi delta in Orissa, Godavari and Krishna deltas in Andhra Pradesh and in Cauvery delta in Tamil Nadu. On the western coast mangroves are found right from Gujarat to Kerala. Andaman and Nicobar Islands have very good growth of mangroves in the sheltered bays and tidal creeks. As per Forest Survey of India data of 1998 a little more than 4800 sq km was under mangrove forests in the country. West Bengal certainly supports the maximum area under mangroves in the Sunderbans. Sunderban mangroves represent the deltaic type of mangrove. The Sunderbans, which covers about 2,109 km^2 area, is reported to contain 30 of the 50 species of the true mangroves in the world. We will deal with the Sunderbans separately on account of its expanse and its environmental importance. The second place is occupied by Andaman and Nicobar according to some experts. Others say Gujarat has a slightly larger area under mangrove than the Andaman and Nicobar Islands. As the mangrove ecosystem develops between land and sea the habitats present there are not of one type. Several distinct types of habitats develop there in the terrestrial environment, aquatic environment and the intertidal region. As far as mangrove flora is concerned there is no anonymity about the species which should be considered as mangrove plants. There are large numbers of plant species which are found in the mangrove region but these are not exclusive to that region. These are found outside the mangrove areas too. On the other hand there are plant species which grow only in the mangrove areas. In all 69 species have been recorded from different mangrove areas of the country. The east coast mangrove areas support 63 of these 69 mangrove species, the west coast has 36 species and 48 species have been recorded from Andaman and Nicobar Islands.

Mangroves are quite rich in terms of faunal diversity too. Wide range of vertebrates and invertebrates are present there. From habitat point of view the animals can be classified into terrestrial and aquatic species. Terrestrial animals include birds, mammals, reptiles, insects, spiders, mites etc. Among these birds have the maximum number of species among the vertebrates inhabiting the mangrove areas. Among the terrestrial invertebrates insects have the maximum number of species. As far as birds are concerned most of the birds use mangrove areas for roosting and as resting place during migrations. In case of mammals maximum numbers of species have been recorded from the Sunderbans. The total number of mammalian species recorded from the Sunderbans goes to forty, including the tiger which is not found in any other mangrove area world over outside the Sunderbans.. Fishes dominate the aquatic fauna. Also, the mangrove areas are rich in zooplanktons and benthic communities. A report prepared by the Zoological Survey of India (ZSI) lists more than 1400 species from the mangrove areas of West Bengal. Andaman and Nicobar Islands is next with more than 900 species. Mangrove areas of Tamil Nadu were found to support more than 800 types of different animals.

Similar to the important role played by tropical rain forests, mangrove ecosystems play a very important environmental role. These areas protect coasts against tides, storms, cyclones etc. The mangrove areas also help in keeping the coastal waters pollution free by absorbing and decomposing the pollutants. In addition, these areas provide safe habitat and breeding ground for different types of animals and birds. Mangrove areas also contribute substantially in the economy of the people living in the coastal areas. People obtain timber, fire wood, fodder, resin etc. from the trees. Honey is collected in large quantity from the mangrove forests. Also, certain plants found in the mangrove ecosystems have medicinal value. In addition to these the mangroves provide habitat and suitable environment for survival and reproduction for certain fish species and molluscs.

Indian coastal areas are known for visits of different types of turtles, especially during the breeding seasons. They visit the sandy shores to lay their eggs. The sight of visiting turtles in large groups provides a spectacular view. Large numbers of people visit egg laying areas every year to enjoy the experience. Bitharkanika in Orissa is one such spot. Olive Ridley turtles visit the area for breeding. Similarly, Leatherback turtles, Green turtles and Hawksbill turtles visit Indian shores for breeding. Sandy shores of Andaman and Nicobar Islands provide nesting grounds to all these four types of turtles.

Globally, the current approaches to the management of coastal resources are not capable of sustainable development. As a result the coastal environments and resources are being rapidly degraded and eroded. The picture relating to management of the coastal zone in India is not very good although for proper utilization and maintenance of the coastal zone, Coastal Zone Regulation Authorities have been constituted for various states and union territories under the Environment (Protection) Act of 1986. Also, a National Coastal Zone Management Authority has been constituted by the central government. However, large areas of mangrove ecosystem have already been destroyed for expansion of cities and towns, for bringing more areas under agriculture, for expansion of industrial activities, for expansion of roads, rail links and facilities for tourists etc. Similarly, corals are being mined for local use or for sale to tourists. Corals are also getting destroyed on account of movement of fishing and other vessels in shallow water. Use of unscientific methods of fishing, discharge of untreated or partially treated effluent, sewage, industrial and municipal wastes in the coastal belts are damaging mangroves, corals and other organisms in substantial way. Similarly, inflow of agriculture chemicals and silt from mainland into coastal ecosystems is damaging them. The impact is evident in the form of death of corals, mangroves and high turbidity and dissolved chemicals in the coastal waters and also in the sediments. All these adversely affect the productivity of the coastal zone and its biodiversity. The immediate impact is being experienced by the fishing communities. Fish catches are declining leading to fall in income.

Now we will describe in short the different regions in India and different types of ecosystems from biodiversity point of view.

1. Forests: As we know the word forest is derived from a Latin word foris which means "out of doors". The word forest hence refers to "a large uncultivated tract of land covered with trees and under wood". As per the assessment done in 2007, forests in the country cover about 21.02% of the total geographical area of the country. The total area works out to 690899 sq. km. In 2005 the area was 690171 sq. km. It means that there was slight improvement in the forest cover within those two years. No doubt the improvement was not very significant. But it indicates towards change that forest area in the country is no more shrinking and it is expanding. This is a positive indication and if the trend continues, biodiversity present in the forest areas will receive better protection and opportunity to expand further. The type of forest in a region depends on the soil properties of the area and the prevalent climatic conditions. Temperature and rainfall the two important factors of climate which determine the forest type in any area. On the basis of the average temperature India can be broadly divided into four distinct zones. These are:

Tropical: very hot and without any winter, the mean annual temperature is over 24°C

Subtropical: hot but with a cool winter, the mean annual temperature is between 17° and 24°C

Temperate: a warm summer and a well defined winter, the mean annual temperature is between 7° and 17°C

Arctic: short summer and a prominent and winter, the mean annual temperature in this region is under 7°C

Forest scientists identify sixteen important types of forests in the country. The same has been endorsed by ICFRE (Indian Council of Forestry Education and Research).

These are as follows:

Tropical forests: The tropical forests are classified into seven types. These are described in short here.

1. **Wet evergreen forests:** These forests are dense and tall. They occur in areas where the rainfall is more than 250 cm per year. These are almost entirely evergreen (where the trees do not shed their leaves at a particular time, leaves are shed all round the year and new leaves are produced simultaneously and the trees remain green all the year round).
2. **The semi-evergreen forests:** These are found in areas where rainfall is from 200 to 250 cm annually. In these forests evergreens as well as deciduous species (which shed all the leaves at a particular time of the year) are found. But the evergreen species dominate.
3. **Moist deciduous forests:** These forests are found in areas with rainfall ranging from 100 to 200 cm annually. They occupy the second place in terms of area among the various types of forests present in the country. They account for more than 30% of the total area of forests in the country. Deciduous species dominate these forests. Evergreen species form the lower storeys. Top canopy of these forests is rarely dense and even. The trees are generally below 25 m in height.
4. **Littoral and swamp forests:** These forests thrive in moist and dry tropical and temperate areas which are associated with wetness. The vegetation is mostly evergreen with variable height and density.
5. **The dry deciduous forests:** These are found in areas with about 100 cm rainfall. This type of forest occupies the maximum area in the Indian forests nearing more than 38% of the total area. The tree vegetation is almost completely deciduous. The trees are generally up to 25m in height. In these forests the ground is covered by grass like vegetation.
6. **Thorn forests:** These forests survive in areas with annual rainfall of less than 50 cm. Trees are generally thorny and less than 10 m in height. The forest floor is generally not covered with grass like vegetation.
7. **The dry evergreen forests:** These forests occupy only about 0.1 % of the total forest area in the country i.e. it occupies the least area in the Indian forests. These forests survive in areas with copious rainfall but with longer dry spells. The vegetation which is generally less than 20 m in height is dominated by hard leaved evergreen trees associated with shrubs and spiny species.

Subtropical forest: The subtropical forests are classified into three types. The three types are described now.

1. Subtropical broad leaved hill forests: These forests are mostly evergreen and as the name suggests. The vegetation comprises of broad leaved species. This kind of forest is found on the hills in the southern part of the country. These forests do not have conifer species. Other species like Eugenia, Gymnosporia, Memecylon, Randia are present in these forests.

2. Subtropical pine forests are found in north-east, in eastern and western Himalayas from 1000 to 2500 m altitude and these forests occupy about 5% of the total forest area in the country.

3. Subtropical dry evergreen forests are found in the foothills of Himalaya in Himachal Pradesh and J & K. The vegetation comprises of scrubs and low xerophytic species.

Temperate forests: Temperate forests are further classified into three types. These are as follows.

1. Montane wet temperate forests: These are evergreen forests. There are no conifers in these forests and the trees grow to height of about 20 m. these forests are found at altitudes more than 1500 m where rainfall is more than 150 cm per annum. Hills in south India and Eastern part of Himalayas have these forests.

2. Himalayan moist temperate forests: These are evergreen forests mainly comprising of conifers and selerophyllus oaks. These forests are also found at altitude of more than 1500 m, in areas where rainfall is from 100 to 150 cm per annum. .

Alpine and sub-alpine forests: These forests are classified in three distinct types which are as follows.

1. Moist alpine scrub: These forests are found above 3000 m height in the Himalayas. The vegetation comprises of dense low scrub.

2. Dry alpine scrub: These forests are open formations consisting of xerophytic scrubs.

3. Sub-alpine forests: These forests are found in the Himalayas above 4500 m to the altitude of 6000 m. The vegetation comprises of evergreen or stunted deciduous species. Generally the vegetation is in close formation. Conifer species may or may not be there.

It is obvious that with so much of variation in the forest types, the floral diversity present there is very rich. Several of the forest types are made of multi-storeys. For example, in case of the Southern tropical wet evergreen forests, which are found in the Western Ghats, the top canopy is Artocarpus, Calophyllum, Depterocarpus, Dysoxylum etc. The second storey is of Cyclstemon, Diospyrus, Elaeocarpus, Hydnocarus, Palaquium and Syzygium. Similarly, several species of bushy genera form the undergrowth in these forests. Then there are different types of climbers and epiphytes. In total the species diversity is very high in these forests. Undoubtedly, the other types of forests are not similarly rich. There are variations. But the total diversity present in the Indian forests is quite high on account of so many types being there and the wide scale of distribution and high degree of variability in the forest types. In our forests and in areas close to the forests we also find several types of trees growing which are indigenous or have been brought from outside. Such common species are Teak, Sal, Chir pine, Blue pine, Deodar, Fir, Spruce, Khair, Shisham, Poplar, Casurina etc.

Faunal diversity of Indian Forests: Indian forests are quite rich in terms of faunal diversity. It is known that faunal diversity in any ecosystem depends on the floral diversity present there. As we have seen earlier the floral diversity of Indian forests is very rich. Also, the geographical as well as environmental characteristics of different forests vary widely. Hence the faunal diversity shows very high level of variation from one region to another. What follows is a short and simple account of the faunal diversity present in different types of forests in the country.

If we look at the evergreen forests, the ground is full of decomposing parts of different types of plants. This situation does not allow many types of animals to survive there. Mostly amphibians and reptiles can successfully survive there. These animals are plenty in there. For example, python, cobras, blind snake, blue throated lizard, tree frogs, Indian Monitor and various species of Caecilians can be easily seen. Among the mammals gaur, elephant, sambar, pig-tailed monkey, phyre's leaf monkey, slender loris, slow loris, tiger, panther, giant squirrels, flying squirrels, porcupine, tree shrew, mole, rats, bats etc. are present. The forests provide plenty of supply of buds, flowers, fruits, seeds, insects and other types of materials which are consumed by the birds and small animals. That is the reason why these forests support high diversity of bird species. The common ones are quails, patridges, wood ducks, baza, pea fowls, hornbills, babblers, sunbird, Fly-catchers etc.

In the semi-evergreen forests, the ground condition is different as adequate sunlight is able to reach the floor of the forests. Due to this the forest floor is full of undergrowth helping various kinds of animals to live and flourish there successfully. For example various types of rodents, deer, civets, otters, wild boar, black bear are commonly found there. Also, large varieties of amphibians and reptiles are also present in these forests. The species composition is similar to what is encountered in the evergreen forests. Among larger species Tiger, elephant, panther, clouded leopard are also found in these forests. Also, Leopard cat is present in these forests and occasionally pangolins are seen.

In case of tropical deciduous forests carnivores like wolf, hyena, jackal, fox, mongoose, civet etc. are commonly found. Elephants, tigers and leopards are also found there. In certain parts of the country four-horned antelope and nilgai (Blue bull) are found in these forests. This type of forest has very rich population of rodents. Birds in this type of forest includes doves, orioles, koels, pigeons, kingfishers, myna, woodpeckers, owls, rollers, bee eaters, hoopoe, bulbuls, tree pies etc. Reptiles are represented by gekko, chameleon, python, cobra, varanus and various other types. Frogs and toads are also there.

The temperate and alpine forests have distinctive fauna. Among the mammals, Brown bear, Snow leopard, Emuine, Panda, Musk deer, Himalayan tahr, Tibetan gazelle, Ibex, Tibetan antelope, Yak, Flying Squirrel etc. are found in these forests. These forests are quite rich in terms of bird flora. Several of them are threatened. Examples are Himalayan monal pheasant, Tibetan blood pheasant, Tibetan snow cock, different species of trogopans etc. this type of forest does not support large number of amphibians and reptiles. However certain types of frogs, lizards, newts, and Caecilian are found there.

The thorn forest and grasslands support certain characteristic species. One horned Rhinoceros is a well known one which is also a threatened species. Nilgiri tahr, pygmy hog are other also threatened. These are found in the grasslands. On account of shrinkage of the grasslands and constant human interference these species are in danger. Indian Cheetah which was also found in the grasslands has already become extinct. We have discussed about this species in detail elsewhere. Wild Ass which is found in the thorn forest of Gujarat is also a threatened species, mainly on account of its shrinking habitat and human interference.

Now we will discuss different regions in the country which form important areas from biodiversity point of view.

1. Eastern Himalayas: Eastern Himalaya spreads to about 2500 km extending from Afghanistan to Pakistan, India, Nepal, Bhutan, and China. Indian Himalaya is from about 250 km to 300 km wide and covers twelve states i.e. J & K, H.P., Uttaranchal, West Bengal, Sikkim, Assam, Arunachal Pradesh, Manipur, Nagaland, Mizoram, Tripura and Meghalaya. Indian Himalayas is generally divided into four zones i.e. Trans-Himalaya, North-West Himalaya, Western Himalaya, and Eastern Himalaya. Eastern Himalaya have been considered as one of the "Hotspots" of biodiversity at international level. This part of the Himalaya consists of plains and hills of different heights and receives abundant rainfall. The climatic conditions vary a lot in this region and the vegetation is extremely rich and all these together result in a wide variety of habitats and ecosystems in the area. There are forests, grasslands, and different types of wetlands. All these result in very rich biodiversity in the region.

If we look at the forests present in the area we find four major types of forests in the region. These are tropical, temperate, sub-alpine and the alpine type of forests. This region receives maximum precipitation and humidity is very high all the year round. Also, on account of its geographical position, this region is in touch with several other floristic regions. As a result the floral diversity is very high in this region. This region is considered to be the one with highest botanical diversity in the entire sub continent. It is not possible to describe the entire floral diversity of the region. We will take up few selected groups of plants to exemplify the floral diversity.

Bamboos: India has 18 genera and 130 species of bamboos. Out of these 15 genera and 82 species are present in the Eastern Himalayas.

Timber yielding species: Large numbers of timber species which provide commercial timber are present in the region. One scientist prepared a list of such species. He could list 35 genera and 37 species, timbers from which are marketed with different names.

Orchids: it is estimated that about 1000 species of orchids are present in India and about 700 species are found in the Eastern Himalayas.

Medicinal plants: The entire Himalayan region has been considered the abode of large number of plants with medicinal properties. In fact many of the manufacturers of formulations of traditional systems of medicine make the claim that rare herbs from Himalayas have been utilized in the formulations. This is done to attract the customers and to prove the efficacy of the formulations. Workers have listed about 100 species of medicinal plants form the region which are in regular trade and use.

Primitive flowering plants: This region is very rich in ancient flowering plants. Several species of such plants are found only in this region and in further eastward areas. One well known example is the several species of Magnolia which are found only in this region and further eastward.

Non-flowering plants: Eastern Himalaya is very rich in ferns and fern-allies. All over India about 1000 species of ferns are found and 50% of them can be found in this region. Several species of ferns found in this region are of rare type. Certain species of Osmunda, Dipteris are the examples. Fern allies like Lycopodium and Selaginella are very well represented in this region. Twelve species of Lycopodium have been reported from there as compared to three from the Western Himalaya.

Faunal diversity: As explained earlier this region has unique geographical location, varied types of habitats and climatic conditions along with large variations in altitude. Also, different types of habitats and ecosystems are present in this region. On account of the same faunal diversity of the region is very high. Also, this region has played very important role in the evolution of the fauna present in the country. It is as this region has always provided passage for entry of faunal species form the other side. The moist evergreen forests of tropical and subtropical types present in this region have always favoured survival of larger number of species and formation of new species through speciation. In this regard only Western Ghats can be compared to a great extent with this region. Rest of the Peninsular India is much poor in terms of ecological conditions to this region.

As far as the listing of faunal diversity of this region is concerned, it is still incomplete to great extent. However, what is already known indicates towards great deal of diversity. Also, the area has high degree of endemism. For example, all the aquatic ecosystems have high degree of fish biodiversity. About 190 species of fishes have been identified from the region from diverse habitats. Out of these more than 40 species are endemic. In terms of Amphibian biodiversity, the Eastern Himalaya is only second to the Western Ghats. In terms of Reptiles the area is quite rich. All the major groups of aquatic reptiles are found in this region. Ten species of turtle and tortoise are there too. Present 40 species of lizards and more than 60 species of snakes have been recorded from these habitats. Among the lizards there are two genera and 35 species which are endemic to the region, Bird fauna of the area is equally rich. More than 45 genera of birds with about 80 species have been recorded from various aquatic habitats in the area. Forests in the region also support high level of bird diversity. Workers have found that about 60% of the total bird species found in the country can be found in the region. In terms of the mammalian fauna the Eastern Himalaya is very rich. About 45% of the Indian mammals are present in this region. The count goes beyond 170 species. A very important species of mammal which is kept in the critical category by the conservationists is found there. It is called Brow antlered deer (Cervus eldi eldi) survives on the floating swamps in the Loktak Lake near Imphal (in Manipur). A large number of threatened mammal species are also found in the region. Some of them are Great one-horned rhinoceros, Hoolock gibbon, Panda, Takin, Phayre's leaf monkey and Pygmy hog. This region has an interesting animal called "Mithan". It is a hybrid between Gaur and the common domestic cattle. This animal is domesticated in the region and used for various purposes.

This region is very rich in terms of wild relatives of cultivated plants too. Those plants are related to species belonging to cereals, millets, legumes, fruits, vegetables, oil seeds, fibre yielding species, spices and condiments etc. Highest number has been recorded for wild relatives of fruit plants and next is the vegetable group. Thus in total the Eastern Himalayas represents a region of very high level of floral and faunal biodiversity.

2. Western Himalayas: It is the smallest among the four regions of the Himalayas covering about 9.6% of the entire Himalayas. It extends to about thirty km in length between the river Kali and the great defile of River Sutlej. Garhwal and Kumaon hills are included in this region. The total area is a little more than 51000 sq km.

Forests of Western Himalayas: On account of variations in soil conditions, topography, geographical location and climate the regions has tropical forest, subtropical forest, temperate forest, alpine and subalpine forests. The tropical forest extends from altitude of 500m 1000m. The subtropical forests extend from 1000m to 2000m. The subtropical forest is divided into broad leaved forest, Pine forest and subtropical evergreen forest. Temperate forests in this region extend from 2000m to 3000m. This type of forest is further divided into broad leaved forest and conifer forest. Subalpine forest is found only above the timberline. It extends from 3400m to 4000m and comprises of stunted bushy plants. Alpine forest in the Western Himalayas extends beyond 4000m and goes up to 5000m where the vegetation ends. Bamboo species, several types of medicinal plants, plants of horticultural importance, orchids etc. are found in abundance in this type of forest. The vegetation of Western Himalayas has a common character. Plants are cold tolerant and drought resistant.

Western Himalayas is very rich in terms of faunal diversity. About 2700 species of animals were listed there few years back. The list included more than 1800 species of invertebrates and about 850 species of vertebrates. Mammals alone from this region account for more than 100 species. There are more than 25 species of bats in this region and 26 species of carnivorous mammals. Few of the carnivorous mammals are tiger, leopard, snow leopard, leopard cat, hyena, sloth bear, black bear, brown bear, jackal, foxes. Five species of deer have been recorded from the region. In addition to these, giant flying squirrel, porcupine and several species of rats and mice can be found in the region.

The Western Himalayas is the home of large number of threatened species of animals and plants. Few of the animals are: caracal, indian fox, himalayan tahr, hog deer, leopard cat, musk deer, jungle cat, leopard, snow leopard, tibetan gazelle, tiger, sloth bear, Himalayan Black Bear and King Cobra etc. Among plants a large variety of medicinal plants have been traditionally obtained from the region. On account of overexploitation many of them are in the list of threatened species. Also, several species of orchids found in the region are traded widely resulting in their disappearance from many places.

3. North-west Himalayas: This region covers the states of Himachal Pradesh and Jammu & Kashmir. But Ladakh, Spiti and Kargil areas are not included in this region as those parts of the two states are included in an independent region called the Trans-Himalayan region. It extends from Pakistan in the western side to Tibet and Central Asia towards the northern side. Altitude in the region varies from 300m to 6000m. More than 50% of the region has altitude beyond 300m. Rainfall in the region varies widely. It ranges from 60mm to 2500mm. Snowfall is also intense in parts of the region. Above 4500m there is perpetual snow while the area above 3000m is covered with snow from December to March extending up to 3m. The North-west Himalayas have several large water bodies. These include fresh water lakes, brackish water lakes and also man-made reservoirs. Some of the natural lakes are Renuka, Khajiar, Rewalsar, Kuneri. Important man made reservoirs formed due to construction of dams are Gobind Sagar, Pong, Pandoh etc. Among these Renuka is very important from ecological point of view as it provides habitat to a large variety of fauna. Main reason is that the lake is located in a remote area and also, it is well protected being situated in the middle of a wildlife sanctuary.

Various rivers drain the area. For example, Jammu & Kashmir is served by the River Indus which has several tributaries including Jhelum, Chenab, Tawi, Zanskar, Nubra etc. Himachal Pradesh is served by five major river systems i.e. Beas, Chenab, Ravi, Sutlej and Yamuna. Another distinctive feature of the region is that large numbers of perennial streams crisscross the area. An important feature of the fauna inhabiting these streams is that they can survive very low temperature, high level of oxygen in water and swift water currents. This is reason that when such streams are disturbed and flow is retarded, for example by damming, the faunal characteristics change and many species just disappear. Even in case of rivers dam construction leads to drastic changes in the ecological characteristics of the rivers leading to disappearance of large number of organisms from the ecosystem.

Pastures occupy more area than any other ecosystem in this region. More than 30% of the total area in Himachal Pradesh and more than 59% in J&K are occupied by permanent alpine pastures. At lower altitudes too there are grasslands in this region. But these are mostly made by the inhabitants by causing deforestation. On the whole the entire region is rich in forage and that is the reason that quite large number of people in the area depend on animal husbandry.

Agro-ecosystems in the region are substantial. Agricultural and horticultural crops are grown there. However, these areas have been created by altering the natural ecosystems originally present there. This change has brought prosperity for the inhabitants but in many places it has resulted in ecological problems. For example, soil erosion has become fast and landslides are quite frequent. Also, flooding in the lower reaches is frequent.

Complete information about the flora of the region is not available. However, it is evident from the available information this not available. However, it is evident from the available information that the floral diversity of the North-west Himalayas is very rich. From the area lying within Kashmir more than 3050 species of flowering plants have been recorded. In case of Kangra valley more than 1000 species of different plants have been recorded. Similarly, more than 1300 species of plants have been documented from the Shimla area. With respect to ferns and other Pteridophytes the North-West Himalayas is very rich. All over India about 350 species of ferns have been identified and in the North-West Himalayas alone about 160 species have been recorded.

Faunal diversity present in the North-West Himalayas is equally rich. Reason is the variety of habitat conditions available in the region. There are different types of forests, variety of soils, large number of lakes and rivers in the region. Also, there are areas covered by snow in the region. All these support a wide range of faunal diversity. For example, in Himachal Pradesh alone 77 species of mammals are found. The area above the snow line supports unique types of mammals. For example, himalayan ibex, tibetan sheep, bharal, wooly hare, snow leopard, himalayan brown bear etc. are found in this region. In the temperate zone we find Leopard cat, Himalayan black bear, Himalayan Tahr, Goral, Musk deer etc. In the lower reaches we can find barking deer, sambar, wild boar, cheetal, common fox, blue bull etc. Animals present in the North-West Himalayas are under variety of threats. Habitat destruction is one of these. Large scale hunting and poaching are other threats to the animals. More than 60 species of animals from this region are in the list of protected species and 25 species are in the highly endangered category. The region is equally rich in terms of birds, reptiles, fish etc. For example about 450 species of birds have been recorded from the region. The region receives large numbers of different species of migratory birds from as far as Siberia, Europe, South-East Asia etc.

4. Trans-Himalayas: The Trans-Himalayas is a distinct bio-geographic region which is generally called as cold desert. The climatic conditions in this region are very harsh. Most of this region is outside India in the Tibetan Autonomous region of China. The Indian portion is mostly in J & K and some in Himachal Pradesh and very small parts are in Uttar Pradesh and Sikkim. The entire Trans-Himalayas covers an area of about 2,600,000 sq. km. Indian portion is about 186,200 sq. km. The topography of the Trans-Himalayas in India is of a plateau interspersed by network of barren mountains. As a result there are deep valleys and high plains. Elevation in the Trans-Himalayas ranges from about 2800m to about 7000m. Various rivers drain the area. Indus drainage system drains most of the Indian Trans-Himalayas. Important tributaries are Zanskar, Shigar, Shyok, Chenab etc. River Spiti is another important river in the area. It merges with the Sutlej river which is a part of the Indus system.

The Ladakh region has very large brackish water lakes. Important ones are Pangong Tso, Tso Morari, Tso Kar etc. Tso Morari provides habitat to large numbers of migratory water fowls. It is the second largest lake in Ladakh with an area of about 138 sq. km. It is situated at altitude of about 4500m. Pangong Tso is another lake in the area which has brackish water and covers about 700 sq.km. About two third of this lake is in Tibet area. Also, fresh water marshes and glaciers are encountered in the Trans-Himalaya. The lakes and other types of wetlands in the region support different types of birds, fishes and other types of aquatic organisms. Most of the wetlands in the Ladakh region are utilized by water fowls as transit spots and breeding grounds. For example, for Barheaded geese and Black-necked crane these serve as the only breeding grounds outside China. Floral and faunal biodiversity of the Trans-Himalaya is very rich. Also, the plants and animals found in this region are unique as they are adapted to severe cold, low atmospheric pressure, high level of solar radiation and extreme aridity.

Vegetation in the Trans-Himalaya is meager, generally is found only in the valleys and in sheltered areas. That is the reason the region is generally barren having sparse natural vegetation. The vegetation in the Ladakh portions ranges from alpine meadows on the mountain slopes to steppe in the valleys. In recent times poplars and willows have been planted along several water courses to provide firewood, construction material and forage. Some experts have classified the natural vegetation in the region into dry temperate forest, sub-alpine forest and dry alpine scrub. edible pine, holm oak, deodar, fir, juniper and rhododendron are found in this region.

Alpine pastures are an important class of ecosystems in the region which provide support to animal husbandry in a big way. These pastures are located a very high altitudes between the tree line and snowline. Variety of grasses, thorny scrub and other types of plants are present in these pastures. These ecosystems add to the biodiversity of the region.

At present there are well developed agricultural areas in the region. But these are not natural. These have been introduced there through clearing of natural vegetation and by developing irrigation facilities to irrigate the desert land which is used for cultivating different types of fruits and vegetables. On account of the same variety of insect pests and their predators can be found there.

As noted above the Indian Trans-Himalaya supports high level of biodiversity and also endemic species on account of its geographical location. For example this region and its adjacent area are considered to be the main centre of origin and evolution of several genera of butterflies. The Changthang region is known globally for preservation of its ungulates and predators. Wild sheep and goats are represented by four species in the region. Also, domesticated ponies, yaks, camels and horses are found there. A rare breed of horse called Zanskari breed can be seen therein the Zanskar valley. Yak is very useful in the area for the inhabitants for carrying load and other purposes e.g. for milk, meat, hide, and wool. A particular type of camel which has double hump is reared in the Ladakh region in the Nubra valley. It is used by the local population for different purposes like transport, riding, polo games etc. The region is very rich in terms of medicinal plants. It is reported that people of the region use about 170 types of medicinal plants for treating different purposes ailments. Also, different species of plants providing fodder, food, forage, fibre, fuel and timber are found in the region. All these add to the biodiversity of the region.

We generally consider that a desert means all sand. But it is not so. A desert may have sand, gravel, bare rock, clay and mud which are sun baked. However, all the deserts have certain common characteristics like low rainfall, land which is arid and expanse of sand, salt or rock which is mostly barren. Only seasonal or sparse vegetation may be found in those areas. The Indian desert is called Thar desert. It occupies more than 2,78,300 sq. km. area. The largest chunk is in Rajasthan where it is also called as Thali. Next is Gujarat and small portions are in Punjab and Haryana. Thar is one of the smallest deserts on the Earth. But it supports a large variety of habitats and those habitats are the abode of rich biodiversity. Another very important feature of the Indian desert is that it is thickly populated. It supports and average density of more than 80 persons per sq.km. Other deserts on the Earth generally support less than 10 persons per sq. km. Also, livestock density is quite high in the Thar. At places it is beyond 225 per sq.km. These factors bring unusual pressure on the biodiversity of the region.

Rainfall in the Thar region is erratic and very little. Monsoon is active in this region from July to September. The average rainfall varies hind s from 100 mm to about 500 mm. Relative humidity is generally low. During summer there are frequent wind storms with speed exceeding 130 km/h. The wind is dry and hot causing desiccation and dehydration. Also, the wind results in shifting of sand dunes frequently. Due to the same only few types of plants are able to settle in the region.

Still Thar is quite rich in terms of biodiversity. Plants adapted to survive there grow and reproduce rapidly as soon as the monsoon sets in. Certain plants have deep roots which spread widely. As soon as there is some rain these roots immediately absorb maximum quantity of water. There are other types of plants which store water in their tissues and do not allow the water to evaporate easily. Common examples are

A one horned rhino and a new born baby. Restricted to a small area and highly endangered.

A wetland, an important component of environment supporting biodiversity

Corals protect the coast and provide habitat to various organisms

Mangrove vegetation protect the coast and provide habitat to various organisms

Natural forest degradation in mountain due to habitation

the cacti. There are still other types of plants which shed the leaves during hot and dry seasons to avoid loss of water through transpiration. Most of the area is occupied by open grassland of dry type interspersed with few trees and thorny bushes. Area occupied by forests is very small. It is less than two percent of the geographical area. But Khejri trees are quite common in the Thar. People inhabiting the area have special consideration for these trees and they protect the trees religiously. Acacia is also commonly found in rocky areas and on low hills. The stabilized sand dunes and plain areas are occupied by mostly shrubs and creepers, which are able to survive there. Most of the animals have developed special adaptations to survive in the harsh climate. They prefer to live in burrows, close to the plant roots, under stones and on leaves of plants. Many of them live in tunnels which are quite long. The animals are mostly nocturnal in habit. During the day they spend their time hiding. The animals have developed special features to control loss of water through evaporation as well. If we talk of numbers, the faunal diversity of Thar represents little more than 2% of the diversity know for the country although Thar occupies about 9% of the geographical area of the country. However we need to remember that the faunal diversity of the Thar has not been worked out very well, especially in case of invertebrates. Scientists are of the opinion that more than 60 to 70 % of the fauna remains to be explored. The available information indicates that Arthropoda represents the largest group and next is the Chordata. In all more than 4500 species have been recorded.

The Thar region supported large populations of several species till recently. But their numbers are dwindling quite fast. A well known example is the Asiatic lion. Another example is the wild ass. These two species are now restricted to Gujarat. Other examples are jungle cat, desert fox, wolf, jackal, hyena and panther etc. which are dwindling fast. Leopard, which used to be quite common in the area, is now seen only rarely. However, black buck and indian gazelle are very common in certain parts of the region. Main reason is that the Bishnoi community considers them sacred and the community protects them religiously. Thar has eleven species of animals including mammals, birds and reptiles which are endemic to the region. In this way Thar is quite important from biodiversity point of view.

Thar is experiencing rapid growth in human population. For example the population of Rajasthan is growing at the rate of about 3% in recent years as compared to the national average rate which is about 1.8%. Also, the population of livestock is growing in the region at fast rate resulting in immense pressure on the grasslands and grazing areas. Mining at large scale and that too in unscientific manner brings additional pressure on the biodiversity present in the region. Indira Gandhi Canal has converted large tracts of desert area into agriculturally productive areas. But at the same time it has changed the environment of the area on account of increased salinity of large areas. In certain areas water logging and flooding are constant menace. These conditions attract and support organisms which were previously not there. For example, malaria has become quite common. Also, agricultural pests previously unknown in the area can be seen there. These developments have brought additional pressures on the biodiversity present in the region.

One of the two hotspots of biodiversity in India lies in the north-east. The unusual physical characteristic of the region has given rise to high ecosystem diversity. As a result, this area supports large number of plant species. All of them have not been studied and documented. On the basis of the available information, the plant diversity of the region can be listed as:

Assam- more than 3000 species,
Arunachal Pradesh- about 4000 species,
Manipur- about 2400 species,
Meghalaya- about 1900 species,
Mizoram- more than 2100 species,
Naglanad- more than 2400 species,
Sikkim and Tripura- about 1500 species.

Now, let us take these states in some more detail.

Assam: Vegetation of Assam is primarily of tropical type, which includes areas of evergreen, semi-evergreen, deciduous forests and grasslands. Along the river banks there are riparian forests as well. In Assam, Poaceae family (grasses) dominates the flora. It accounts for more than 200 species. Next is Orchidaceae with about 195 species. Also, large numbers of medicinal plants have been recorded from Assam. Although the list is not yet complete, about 350 species of plants with known medicinal uses have been reported from Assam. Assam is rich in terms of bamboo diversity. Forty two species of bamboos have been recorded in Assam. Assam is also the store house of large number of rare and endangered plants. Although the listing is far from complete, 60 species of plants which are rare, endangered or threatened have been recorded by various workers. Assam has large number of fungi, algae, lichens, pteridophytes and gymnosperms which are used as food by the local population.

The rich diversity of Assam is reflected in animals as well. Large number of species of primates, herbivores, carnivores and birds are found in Assam. More than 190 species of mammals and about 960 species and subspecies of birds are known to occur there. If we take into account only the primates, 14 species are present in the state and they represent 1/6th of all the primates present in the world. Assam is well known for its Indian one-horned rhinoceros. About 75 percent of the total world population of this endangered animal is found in Assam. Assam is equally rich in terms of fish diversity. More than 185 species of fishes have been recorded so far. There are 10 species of fresh water snails which are used as food by the tribal population of the state. In case of butterflies, about half of the total species present in India are present in Assam.

Arunachal Pradesh: Arunachal is in the eastern Himalaya and it is part of one of the twenty five hotspots of biodiversity on the earth. The range of ecosystems present in the state is very wide from hot and humid tropics to alpine meadows. Twenty types of forests have been recorded from the state. Consequently, we find one of the richest species diversity in Arunachal. As far as floral diversity is concerned, more than 4500 species of flowering plants and 400 species of pteridophytes have been recorded from the state. Similarly, 33 species of gymnosperms, 45 species of bamboo, more than 50 species of Rhododendron, 600 species of orchids and about twenty species of canes have been recorded. More than 500 species of plants found in the state are used in traditional medicine. A large number of rare and endangered plants are present in the state. Common examples are Tetracentron sinensis, which is an angiosperm but without vessels, Magnolia campbelli, a primitive angiosperm, Dischidia rafflesiana, with leaf pitcher etc. The state is quite rich in wild relatives of cultivated plants. These belong to cereals, millets, legumes, oil seeds, vegetables, fruits, fibres, spices etc. All this information relates to only about 60 percent of the area of the state which has been explored so far.

With respect to fauna as well Arunachal is quite rich. Four major cats i.e. tiger, leopard, snow leopard and clouded leopard are found in the state. Other types of cats like fishing cat, leopard cat, golden cat, marbled cat are also found here. It is the only state which supports three goat antelopes. These are goral, takin and serow. Arunachal is the only state where seven species of primates, including hoolock gibbon and slow loris are present. About 2000 elephants are there in the state. They have common corridors with Assam and Bhutan and probably also with Myanmar. Musk deer, an endangered species has also been reported from Arunachal in addition to three other species of deer.

In conclusion, it can be said that the north east part of India is extremely rich from biodiversity point of view. Large number of plant and animal species are present there and many of them are endemic. Also, large numbers of species are endangered. All this information is based on limited surveys conducted in the area. Intensive efforts are required to conserve and protect the rich biodiversity of the region.

Manipur: On account of its physical features and its inclination towards south, Manipur has variety of climatic conditions which result in different types of forests being present in the state. These range from tropical to sub-alpine. There are two major rivers (Barak and Chindwin) and thirteen major lakes in Manipur which add to the variety of ecological conditions resulting in richness of biodiversity. About 500 species of orchids, more than 50 bamboo species, about 160 fish species, several Asian mammals, large number of moths and butterflies are found in Manipur. Manipur is quite rich in medicinal plants. Certain reports suggest the existence of more than 150 types of medicinal plants, while others claim the number to be about 450. The brow antlered deer (*Cervus eldi eldi*) found in Manipur in the Keibul Lamjao National Park is highly endangered. The state of Manipur represents an important center of origin of a variety of flowering plants. Also, Manipur has a large percentage of plants which are endemic.

The cultural, religious and traditional beliefs and rites of ancient Manipur are associated with the love and care for wildlife. For example, it was believed that a prince of Luwang clan transformed himself into the Sangaideer. A village girl, who could not bear the torture of her stepmother, became a hornbill. Similarly, every clan has some fish or vegetable 'not to be eaten' and every village has the tradition to maintain a sacred grove for worship of god/goddess called Umanglai/ Umanglairembi. On auspicious occasions like new year, marriage etc. some fish, cock or bull were released. Recapturing of such animals is forbidden.

Meghalaya: Different parts of Meghalaya have wide variation with respect to topography, soil properties, climatic conditions, rain fall etc. In Meghalaya, rains are torrential for about five months starting from May to September. Meghalaya is well known for rain records. Cherrapunjee and Mawsynram receive highest rainfall in the world. During last about two decades, rainfall at Cherrapunjee has been from 11995 mm to 14189 mm while at Mawsynram the rainfall was from 10689 to 13802 mm. Also, the geographical position of Meghalaya is quite unique which could favour introduction of plant species from neighbouring states as well as from Tibet, China and Myanmar. All these factors have led to rich biodiversity for the state. As far as vegetation is concerned, Meghalaya has a wide variety ranging from tropical and sub-tropical to temperate and near temperate.

From faunal diversity point of view, Meghalaya is quite rich. It has about 5600 known species. This is quite high when we take into account the total number for India i.e. about 90000 species. In case of birds, more than 540 species, i.e. about 50 percent of birds found in India, have been recorded from this state. In case of mammals, more than 35 percent of Indian species (total: 139) are present in Meghalaya. Similarly, with respect to other groups as well Meghalaya is quite rich. More than 90 species of reptiles, 150 of fish and 33 of amphibians have been recorded from Meghalaya. A good number of these are endangered and many of them are endemic.

Mizoram: This state shows enormous diversity of ecosystems and geographical conditions which has resulted in rich biodiversity. However, the biodiversity of the state is not properly recorded on account of various problems. But, more important is that biodiversity of Mizoram is suffering loss on account of hunting, overexploitation, habitat loss, introduction of exotic species and social factors like disruption of traditional Mizo management system etc.

Forests of Mizoram are classified under three types, tropical wet-evergreen forests, tropical semi-evergreen forests and montane sub-tropical pine forests. Among these, the wet-evergreen forests are the most important from production point of view. This type of forest is rich in Terminalia myriocarpa(Hollock), Dipterocarpus turbinates(Gurjan), Amoora wallichii, Michelia champaca (Champa), Artocarpus chaplasha (Chaplash) etc. According to one report more than 400 ethnomedicinal plants could be recorded from Mizoram. Similarly, twenty species of bamboo have been reported from different areas of the state.

Faunal diversity of Mizoram has not been worked out properly. However, it is expected that the state is very rich in this respect. In one study it was reported that more than 225 species of birds belonging to 50 families were present there. Historically, Mizoram was quite rich in terms of wild animals. However, due to uncontrolled hunting, shifting cultivation etc., the population of wild animals has come down drastically. Now, they can be found only in the interior of the forests and authentic information about these animals relating to population, diversity etc. is not available.

Sikkim: This Himalayan state is characterized by vast altitudinal variations within short distances. The variations range from 300 m to more than 8500 m. This is the reason that in the Rangeet Valley there are Sal forests while in the north there are temperate forests. Vegetation of Sikkim can be divided into five altitudinal zones. These are tropical zone, the subtropical zone, the temperate zone, alpine forest and scrub, and the trans-Himalayas. Sikkim is quite rich in medicinal plants, wild flowers and vegetables, mushrooms, wild fruits, nuts, rhododendrons, spices, seasoning, timber trees, fodder trees, grasses, lichens, mosses, algae etc. Among animals, Barking deer, Leopard, Langur, Goral, Bear, Musk deer, Snow leopard, Wolf, Fox, Jackal, Wild dog etc. are found in Sikkim. Sikkim is rich in fish species too. Twenty two wild species of fish are found in the state. Similarly, large number of species of butterflies, moths, honey bees, wild silk moths are found in Sikkim. It is claimed that the Europeans carried the seeds of Rhododendrons from Sikkim to grow in their own countries. Rhododendron is now grown extensively in certain parts of Europe and it has resulted in extensive economic activity in the region.

Tripura: Tripura's forest is classified as tropical forests. There are evergreen forests, moist deciduous forests, bamboo forests, garjan forests, cane breaks, savannahs and grassland. Different varieties of wild animals are found in Tripura. This richness is on account of the bio-geographical location of the state. Ninety species of land mammals have been recorded from this state. Fifteen species of primates are found in India and seven of these are present in Tripura. Several species found in Tripura are highly endangered. Common examples are Hoolock gibbon, Slow lorris, Phyre's langur. Tripura is equally rich in birds, amphibians, reptiles, fishes and different types of invertebrates.

Tripura is quite rich in fruits and spices. More than 60 fruit crops are found in the state and these crops show great deal of genetic variability. For example, there are 28 genetic variables of jackfruit in the state. With respect to algae, fungi, bryophytes and pteridophytes too, Tripura is very rich. About 20 species of edible mushrooms have been reported from the state.

Western Ghats: ***The Poet Kalidas described the hills of Western Ghats as a pretty damsel. Her head lies towards Kanyakumari, her feet braced against Satpura hills. She wears a green sari of verdant rain forests.***

Western Ghats or Sahyadris is the hill chain which runs parallel to the west coast of India for about 1400 km covering an area of about 1,40,000 sq. km. They pass through

Gujarat, Maharashtra, Goa, Karnataka, Kerala and Tamil Nadu. It ends at Kanyakumari in Tamil Nadu. They range from a relatively narrow strip of coast on the western side to hills reaching height of about 2800 m. After that the Western Ghats merge with the Deccan Plateau in the east.The Western Ghats is part of the Indo-Malayan bio-geographical zone and it is divided into two biotic provinces- the Malabar coasts/plains and the mountains. The average width of the Western Ghats range to about 100 km. There are large numbers of high peaks in the region and most of them are more than 1400 m high. Another important feature of the Western Ghats is that they are isolated from other moist formations by prevailing drier climatic conditions in the surrounding areas. On the western side is the sea, Vindhyas and Satpura ranges are towards north and the arid Deccan plateau towards the east. This isolation and resulting insulation has resulted in the process of speciation leading to large numbers of endemic species, in both the groups i.e. flora and fauna. Also, we find large number of examples of vacariance. It refers to the formation of different sister species derived from a common ancestor. At present the sister species are considered separate species. One of them is found in the evergreen forests of the Western Ghats and the other in the adjacent dry regions. Obviously, the species so derived and living in the Western Ghats becomes endemic to the region. There are about 1500 plant species in the Western Ghats which are endemic to the region. Even otherwise the Western Ghats region is extremely rich in species and is one of the twenty hot spots of biodiversity on the earth. Wild relatives of many economically important plants like Musa, Oryza, Piper, Zingiber, Curcuma, Dioscorea etc. are found in abundance in the region. In terms of faunal diversity too there are two main centers of diversity in the region. These are Agasthyamlai hills and the Silent Valley. Silent Valley is one of the last surviving stands of rainforest in South India. Silent Valley had attained international fame in the 1970s on account of a proposal to dam the river Kunthi which passes through Silent Valley. On account of construction of the dam a large portion of virgin rainforest was to be submerged and destroyed. There was large scale protest against the plan which later turned into a countrywide movement. The government had to respect people's sentiment and the plan was shelved. As a result the forest was saved. Probably, it was the first victory of people's sentiments related to environment in the country after Independence. Now, the same forest forms the Silent valley National Park. The richness of species and genera in the region and the high incidence of endemic species together with the threats being faced by the region on account of human interference have placed the Western Ghats as one of the 25 Hot Spots of biodiversity on the Earth.

Most of the major rivers of Southern Peninsular India and their tributaries originate in the Sahyadri Ranges. For example, Godavari originates near Nasik, Krishna's largest tributary, Bhima originates near Mahabaleshwar and Cauvery originates in Coorg area.

The Peninsular rivers are dependent on monsoons. Climate of Western Ghats is mainly monsoonal. The rainy season is between June and September. The rainfall in the region varies from 100 to 500 cm or even more going up to 850 cm or so. This situation has resulted in extremely humid climate in the region with very short spells of dry season. There are three types of soil in the Western Ghats region. These are red soils, black soils and lateritic soil. All these and other associated factors have resulted in great deal of variation with respect to vegetation in this region. There are grasslands, scrub jungles, dry and moist deciduous forests, semi-evergreen and wet evergreen forests. A recent attempt by experts distinguish nineteen floristic types according to altitude, eight types in low elevation, five at medium elevation and three at high elevation. From flora point of view the Western Ghats is one of the richest areas in the country. Almost one-third of all the flowering plant species found in India numbering about 3500 are present in this region. In case of lower plants too, the Western Ghats is equally rich. If we take the example of tree species alone, we find that representatives of families starting from Anacardiaceae, Annonaceae, to Sterculiaceae and Theaceae are present in the Western Ghats. In all, tree species representing more than forty families have been recorded from the region. Dalbergia genus which includes the rosewood has twenty five species spread all over India. Out of these 22 are present in the Western Ghats. Similarly, the Western Ghats has 84 species of orchids. Three genera of orchids are endemic to the Western Ghats. Also, the area shows high degree of endemism. Around 40 percent of plants present in the region are endemic. Another study has brought out that about 63 percent of tree species in the low and medium evergreen forests of the Western Ghats are endemic. In all Western Ghats has about 1500 species of plants which are endemic to the region. Another interesting fact about the region is that wild relatives of large numbers of economically plants are found in abundance in the region. Common examples are Musa, Oryza, Piper, Curcuma and Zingiber. In terms of orchids the Western Ghats is very rich. More than 80 species of orchids are found there. More than one third of all the orchids found in the Peninsular India is endemic to the Western Ghats.

In case of faunal diversity too, the region is very rich. However, information about the invertebrates is not adequate while the vertebrates have been studied in more detail. Western Ghats has more than 200 species of freshwater fishes. About 120 of them are endemic to the region. In terms of amphibians the region is richest in the country. About 220 species of animals belonging to this group are known to occur in India and more than 130 species are found in the Western Ghats. More importantly, more than 100 of these are endemic to the Western Ghats. Two of the species found in the Western Ghats are listed in the Red Data Book. Interesting examples are the Torrent frogs. Seven species of this frog are found in the Western Ghats region. All of these seven species are endemic to the region. In terms of birds the Western Ghats has about 350 species or subspecies. Hornbills of several types, Racket tailed drongos, Fairy blue birds etc. are commonly found in the region. Spot-billed pelican (Pelecanus philippensis) and Florican (Eupodotis indica) found in the region are globally threatened. More than 70 of these are endemic to the region. Common examples are Nilgiri wood pigeon, Malabar grey hornbill, Grey headed bulbul, Rufous babbler and Malabar parakeet. Among animals as well there are endemic species. In terms of mammal species too the Western Ghats is quite rich. More than 105 species belonging to about 75 genera are present in the region. A number of the mammal species (12 in all) found there are endemic to the region. The Western Ghats provides habitat to large number of species of larger animals like Elephant, Tiger Gaur, Dhole (wild dog), Sloth bear, Panther and several species of deer, including the Barking deer and

Sambar deer are found there. In addition Nilgiri langur, Lion-tailed macaque, Giant squirrel are also present in the region. Chousinga, a small antelope is also found in the Western Ghats. Males in this species have two pairs of horns, which gives the animal its name which literally means 'four horned'. Similarly, the bird fauna of the region is very rich.

Taking into account the rich biodiversity of the Western Ghats region a number of protected areas have been created there. Few of the important ones are the Borivali National Park near Mumbai, Nagarhole National Park, Bandipur National Park, Annamalai Wildlife Sanctuary, Periyar National Park and Silent Valley National Park. On account of the declaration of the protected areas in the region a substantial chunk of flora and fauna is receiving protection. Otherwise, during the past about six decades the biodiversity of the region has suffered due to mining, urbanization, development of infrastructures, industrialization and similar other types of developmental activities. Large tracts of the natural ecosystems have been cleared or converted into agricultural and horticultural areas. Tea, coffee and rubber plantations have eaten upon large areas of natural forests in the region. This is the reason that forest clearing and human encroachment have been identified as the major threats in the region. Illegal poaching of wild animals and overexploitation of plant resources such as those having medicinal value or direct economic value like orchids have aggravated the situation further. But we cannot underestimate the importance of the remaining areas from biodiversity point of view. The same need to be protected if we are interested in preserving the unique biodiversity present in the region. Otherwise we will lose the rich biodiversity of the Western Ghats which would mean a substantial part of the entire country's biodiversity.

The great Indian hornbill lives here and grows to a length of about 1.4 m. It has black and white body with a large yellow bill. On the top of the bill there is a hornlike casque made of solid ivory. The name hornbill is related to the horn on the bill.

The Eastern Ghats: Generally while discussing the biodiversity of India the Eastern Ghats region is not given adequate importance and it is ignored although biologically, the Eastern Ghats is one of the floristic zones of India. The total number of such floristic zones is nine. Thus Eastern Ghats is one of the nine floristic zones of the country. Reason for it being generally ignored is that the Eastern Ghats is a group of isolated hills, plateaus, gorges, basins and ranges etc. which do not provide a continuous habitat dissimilar to the Western Ghats. The altitude in the Eastern Ghats ranges from almost sea level to about 1750 m. Several rivers like Cauvery, Godavari, Krishna, Pennar, Mahanadi pass through the Eastern Ghats before flowing to the Bay of Bengal. On account of the activities of these rivers the Eastern Ghats has large number of cuts as well as waterfalls, gorges etc. The Eastern Ghats has tropical monsoon climate and it receives rain during south west monsoon and north east monsoon. Rainfall in the region varies from 600 mm to 1600 mm. Mean temperature in the region remains between 20°C and about 40°C. During the winter the night temperature may dip to about 2°C.

Vegetation present in the Eastern Ghats shows large degree of variation. Evergreen forests, Tropical semi-evergreen forests, Tropical moist deciduous forests, Southern tropical dry deciduous forests, Northern mixed dry deciduous forests, Dry savannah forests, Tropical dry evergreen forests and Tropical dry evergreen scrub are present in the region. On account of presence of these forest types the region is quite rich in plant diversity. More than 2500 species of flowering plants (angiosperms) have been recorded from the region.

Animal diversity present in the Eastern Ghats is not as rich as in the Western Ghats. However, in its own way Eastern Ghats too supports large varieties of animals. For example more than 110 species of amphibians and reptiles have been reported from the region. Similarly, about 300 species of birds have been recorded from the region and chances are that with time more types of birds may be found in the region. Certain species of birds which were considered extinct have been found in the region. In terms of mammals too, the region is quite rich. For example, the cat family alone is represented by tiger, leopard, jungle cat. Also, Striped hyena, Fox, Jackal, Indian wild dog, sloth bear, chowsingha, blue bull are found in the region.

The Eastern Ghats region is experiencing different types of stress. Deforestation is an important factor. Large areas of forests have been cleared in the region for agriculture, mining, industry, urbanization, development of transport and other infrastructures etc. A special type of shifting cultivation called "Podu" has resulted in large scale changes in the flora and fauna in the region. This practice is quite old. But in recent time the cycle of shifting cultivation has become very short which does not allow sufficient time for regeneration. Result is that larger areas get degraded with passing years. Unprecedented growth in population in the region is an important factor. Large scale utilization of bamboo from forests for industrial use has changed the complexion of natural forests. Construction of dams and canals in the region has brought additional pressure on the biodiversity of the region. There is need for urgent measures to conserve the natural habitats in the region and associated flora and fauna. Otherwise the entire area may turn barren in near future.

The Sunderbans: The Sunderbans represent the world's largest delta formed by three rivers, Ganga, Brahmputra and Meghna. The name Sunderbans comes from the dominant tree species locally called 'Sundari'. Scientifically, the tree is Heritiera fomes. The delta is spread over about 80000 sq. km. The mangrove forests of Sunderbans are spread over about 10000 sq. km., 40 percent of which is in India and the rest in Bangladesh. It also represents the largest estuarine forest on the earth. This huge tidal swamp forest, consisting mainly of mangroves, is spread over an area of about 2500 sq. km. There are islands, swamps and forests which are interwoven with a network of rivers and rivulets. The larger channels are about one and half km. in width while the smaller ones are just like drains. On account of these water channels half of the Sunderbans remains submerged under water. The rest of the area is covered by low lying islands and mud-banks with sandy beaches and dunes along the coast. Rainfall in Sunderbens area is heavy. On several occasions the mean annual rainfall has been recorded to be around 2000 mm. Humidity is always high in the area remaining around 80 percent on average. Monsoon starts from middle of June and continues to middle of September.

The mangrove forest on the Indian side is about 4300 sq. km. Little more than half of it is forest and the rest is water. The forests in Sunderbans are classified as moist tropical seral forest consisting of beach and tidal forests. In the early 20th century, scientists listed more than 330 species of plants from the area. Recently, the species composition of the mangrove vegetation was worked out and about 70 species were listed. The mangrove vegetation of Sunderbens and other locations on the east coast are luxuriant and diverse as the rivers like Ganga, Godavari, Krishna, Cauvery and Mahanadi etc. bring large supplies of freshwater and nutrients to the deltas formed by the rivers. Also, in terms of other types of flora the Sunderbens is quite rich. For example, Sunderbens has more than 45 species of phytoplankton.

The faunal diversity of Sundarbens is still very rich although the Sundarbens has lost several species on account of loss of habitat and increased salinity in the area. Examples are Jaavan rhinoceros, Water buffalo, Swamp deer, Indian muntjac, Gharial. Sundarbens has the largest tiger population in the country (more than 260). A distinct feature of the tigers in Sundarbens is that a large number of them have turned man eaters. Another characteristic of the tigers is that they have adopted themselves to saline aquatic environment and they are good swimmers. It is claimed that the tigers turn man eaters on account of constant encounter with the saline environment. Also, lack of adequate number of prey animals has forced them to become man eaters. Several types of dolphins are also found in the area. A variety of reptiles (58 species) are found in the Sundarbens. Common examples are olive ridley turtles, estuarine crocodile, monitor lizard, river terrapin, Indian python. creeks of Sunderbens provide spawning ground to about 90 species of fish, about 50 species of crabs and several types of Molluscs. The Sundarbens area is quite rich in terms of birds. Common examples are several types of storks, a variety of kingfishers, several species of egrets, eagles, terns, ducks, herons etc. In all more than 1400 species comprising different groups of animals have been recorded from the Sunderbens area. More than 175 species of fishes and more than 160 species of birds have been recorded from the area. Forty species of mammals have also been recorded from the area.

In conclusion, it can be said that India is extremely rich in terms of biodiversity. This is obvious from **Tables 2** and 3, which provide information about recorded number of species of plants and animals in India and compare the same with the numbers recorded globally.

□□□

CHAPTER 8

Need to Conserve Biodiversity

We need to understand that ecosystems survive because plants, animals and microorganisms are present there i.e. on account of the biodiversity present there. If these are not there the non-living components of the ecosystems cannot complete the ecosystems. Obviously, the services provided by ecosystems are primarily due to the presence of plants, animals and microorganisms.

Efforts have been made by scientists to identify various goods and services provided by ecosystems. There is a long list of items which we obtain from different ecosystems and of the services rendered by the ecosystems on their own. The important ones include:

- Food, fuel, fibre, rubber, oil etc.
- Shelter and building materials,
- Medicines, and other products,
- Purification of air and water,
- Detoxification and decomposition of wastes,
- Stabilization and moderation of the Earth's climate,
- Moderation of floods, droughts, temperature extremes and the forces of wind,
- Nutrient cycling and generation and renewal of soil fertility,
- Pollination of plants, including crops,
- Control of pests and diseases,
- Storehouse of genetic resources which are used as inputs for generating new varieties and for improving existing crop varieties and livestock breeds,
- Cultural, spiritual and aesthetic benefits,
- Knowledge and educational benefits.

We can easily understand that the benefits that we obtain from the ecosystems or the services that the ecosystems provide are on account of the biodiversity present there. For example, if we take the case of pollination, a large numbers of plants including the crops and fruit plants are pollinated by insects like honey bee, butterflies, moths etc. They are there as components of the biodiversity. Similarly, plants absorb nutrients from soil and then the nutrients become available to animals and other organisms. Finally, the nutrients are brought back to soil by the detritovores and decomposers by way of decomposition of the waste materials, discarded body parts and remains of plants and animals. There are certain plants which convert gaseous oxygen into chemical compounds and add it to soil. Other plants and animals use the same nitrogen compounds to meet their nitrogen requirements.

GRASSES

It is the name given to the members of one family of plants. The family is Gramineae or Poaceae. Its members are commonly called grasses.

This family is one of the most recently evolved families of the flowering plants. But this family represents the third largest family consisting of about 10000 species of plants. Members of this family range from very small plants found in the alpine pastures to very tall bamboos.

Grasses are intimately related to human needs and survival. Most of the grains we eat every day are seeds of grasses. Common examples are rice, wheat, millets, maize etc. Even sugarcane which provides us most of the sugar is a grass.

We know that most of the herbivores depend on different types of grass in the form of forage and fodder. We use grass for making roofs, walls, floors, doors, baskets, thatching, variety of handicraft items, and it is also used as fuel by very large number of people in the developing and underdeveloped countries.

Ecologically too, grass is extremely important. Their roots effectively hold soil protecting it against wind and water erosion. Grass covering on soil helps percolation of rainwater by retarding their flow and keeping the surface soil soft and porous. Thus its presence is very helpful in enriching the underground water table.

Grasses can grow in almost all types of environment ranging from nutrient poor soil to saline environment, in water logged conditions or even in heavily polluted conditions. These species are extremely efficient in withstanding pressure from grazing, trampling and also fire. They regenerate as soon as the pressure is reduced or finished. That was the reason that famous Urdu poet Iqbal wanted people to learn important lesson from grasses. Even if these are crushed, they are not finished. They remain alive, regenerate and start growing no sooner than the pressure is gone. Grasses help improve the soil condition by adding more humus than other types of plants. This is the reason that grasses are the first among flowering plants that establish in barren areas and on wastelands. Subsequently other types of plants including trees are able to establish there, completing the process of succession.

We need to realize that if members of only one family of plants i.e. grasses can contribute so much to our well being, how much the entire plant kingdom may be doing for us.

We know that biodiversity present in oceans and seas is decreasing fast. There is urgent need to protect the biodiversity there. This is possible by protecting the marine habitats. But it will involve huge costs. No country is ready to bear the same. For example, it has been estimated that a network of marine protected areas to conserve 20%-30% of the seas and oceans may cost between $5bn and $19bn. It is huge amount of money. But if we look at the benefits it can bring, we will be convinced that the investment will not be out of place. For example, this kind of investment can safeguard $70bn to $80bn worth of fish catches. In addition, the investment will ensure continuation of marine ecosystem services valued at \$4.5 to \$6.7 trillion annually. The problem is that who will bear the cost. After all, no country or organization owns an ocean or a sea. It is likely that in future various countries cooperate and invest in this kind of environmental ventures.

We are aware of the fact that mangrove areas all over the world are dwindling fast. Reasons are well known and we have discussed this elsewhere. Globally, how much mangrove areas contribute towards fisheries has not been estimated. However, in one study it came out that the annual economic median value of fisheries supported by mangrove habitats in the Gulf of California was about \$37,500 per hectare. Similarly, the contribution of mangroves in coastal protection has been estimated to be as much as \$300,000 per km of the coastline. If we consider the entire mangrove areas, the total contribution will be astounding. Still, we are destroying the mangroves for quick gains which by any standard cannot match the long term contribution made by the mangrove areas.

We know that lot of people visit Africa as tourists. Main attraction is the natural diversity present there and the associated wildlife. Innumerable films and TV programmes are produced annually on subjects related to the environment and wildlife of Africa. It provides income to the local administration. Also, the local population is benefited by way of payments made for local assistance, hospitality etc. the films and TV programmes are viewed by millions of persons all over the world and they get interested in visiting the continent. It has been estimated that in Africa nature related tourism generates approximately the same amount of revenue as farming, forestry and fisheries combined together. Obviously, if the natural resources are allowed to degenerate, tourism industry will suffer leading to loss in revenue.

Recently the greatest worry of the entire world is the growing carbon dioxide level in the atmosphere which is leading to global warming and climate change. We know that green plants absorb carbon dioxide. Forests play very important role in this process as the forests are full of greenery. Right from the small plants at ground level to the top of the tallest trees photosynthesis is performed. Consequently, carbon dioxide is absorbed from the atmosphere and stored in the form of biomass. Not much authentic data is available for the carbon dioxide absorbed by forests in different parts of the world. However, occasional authentic estimates have been made. For example, the national parks of Canada are estimated to store 4.43 gigatonnes (billion metric tonnes) of carbon, a service worth at least \$11bn. Its value may extend to \$2.2 trillion depending on the price of carbon in the market. The protected areas of Mexico store 2.45 gigatonnes of carbon dioxide every year. This quantity is more than five years of Mexico's carbon dioxide emissions as estimated in 2004. In money terms it is valued at \$12.2 billion. Although the quantities of carbon dioxide absorbed and stored by forests in other parts of the globe have not been worked out in detail, we can easily understand value of the same. At this point we must understand that this is only about one role that the forests play i.e. carbon storage. The other roles of forests are additional. If we take into account all the contribution value will be astronomical. For example, a report in 2003 estimated the total value of annual benefits of the United Kingdom's forests to its people to be around £1 billion. They included recreation (£393 m), biodiversity (£386 m), landscape (£150 m) and carbon sequestration (£94 m). The estimate, carried out by Britain's Forestry Commission, did not include values such as the contribution of forests to the supply and quality of fresh water, the cleansing of pollutants from the air, and reduction of soil erosion. If these are added the contribution will become much more impressive. Another example is of the Great Barrier Reef of Australia. It is estimated to contribute nearly 6 billion Australian Dollars to the country's economy in terms of tourism, other recreational activities and commercial fishing. If other roles played by the reef are taken into consideration, the amount may grow several times.

We know about India that a large number of tourists come from outside just to see the wildlife present here. For example, tigers in India are a big attraction for people living in other countries. People travel to Kanha, Ranthambore, Pench, Jim Corbett, Suderbans etc. to see the tiger in the wild. Earlier Sariska, which is close to Delhi attracted large number of tourists. Few years back it was reported that Sariska lost all the tigers on account of poaching. From then onwards not many tourists visit Sariska. People from all ov er the world visit Gir in Gujarat to view Asiatic lion in wild. Gir is the only place in the world where these lions can be seen in wild. Similarly, tourists from all over the world travel to Assam and adjoining areas to see the one-horned rhino in the wild. Bharatpur Bird Sanctuary is visited by large number of people every year on account of the birds present there. Tourists in large numbers visit Ladakh, Himachal Pradesh, Uttaranchal, and North-east etc. on account of the natural beauty and biodiversity present there. Jodhpur, Jaisalmer, Bikaner etc. in Rajasthan are visited by thousands of tourists each year just on account of the unique ecosystems and the associated biodiversity in the area. Now white tiger is present in different zoos of several countries. All these tigers have their origin in India in a small place called Gobindgarh, near Rewa in Madhya Pradesh. In May 1951, a unique tiger cub was captured from the forest near Rewa and it was brought to the palace of ruler of Rewa at Gobindgarh. There it was kept in the palace and named Mohan. There Mohan lived with different tigresses and produced several white cubs. In June 1963 a pair of white tigers was transferred to Delhi Zoo from Gobindgarh. Till then not many people knew about the existence of white tigers as they were living in seclusion in Gobindgarh. Once the pair reached Delhi, not only people from surrounding areas but also from far off places visited Delhi Zoo to have a glimpse of the white tigers. At that time there was no TV. Hence, people could not see the tigers if they did not travel to Delhi. It may surprise many people that large number of people from other countries came to Delhi just to see the white tigers. This trend continued for months. Later white tigers were gifted to other countries by the government of India. Presently all the white tigers in different zoos in India and abroad are progenies of Mohan.

Certain initiatives associated with tourism and wildlife management have proved quite successful in the past years in the country. For example, at Periyar Wildlife Sanctuary an Eco-development Committee was formed involving local people who were earlier engaged in sandalwood smuggling, poaching and illegal removal of bark from cinnamon trees. Pending cases against those persons were withdrawn. In return they started protecting the forests. Now they also provide services to tourists and earn reasonable income. In Tamil Nadu at Kumbhakarnan Falls more than hundred tribals are working as tourist guides, called eco-guards, after receiving proper training. These tribals also regulate the tourist traffic and maintain the area in accordance with ecotourism guidelines. In return the fee collected from tourists is provided to them. In Sunderbans, the villagers are participating in ecotourism programme. They provide accommodation and food to visiting tourists. A number of the young villagers have been trained to act as guides. Their services have been made mandatory for the tourists visiting the area. In return to various services the villagers receive substantial income. As a result they have developed stake in sustainable tourism in the area. It is essential that with in future such initiatives must be encouraged in other areas to help in conservation of resources, including biodiversity present in different areas of the country.

Considering the importance of biodiversity, the UN Convention on Biological Diversity has recognized that biodiversity is important for maintaining life-sustaining systems. This conclusion is based on the observation that areas rich in clean water, fertile soils and high quality forests are also rich in species. Areas which are degraded, polluted and unproductive, generally supports low level of biodiversity. This way the biodiversity remains an integral part of the life-support system. As already discussed, the biodiversity is dynamic at all levels. Ecosystems may disappear, certain species may vanish and new species may appear. However, in nature all this happens in slow pace and in a systematic manner. This is the reason that the Earth's biodiversity never faced any big threat during thousands of years. But, in recent times, the human being has brought changes in this pattern. It has triggered the process which lead to extinction and it has played important role in disappearance of a large number of species within short time. We will discuss this aspect in detail later. However, we need to understand that if this trend continues, the Earth will be devoid of its rich diversity quite soon. Hence, it is time to take action to conserve and protect the diversity present on the Earth. This is possible only if we understand the value of biodiversity. IUCN lists some of the benefits and threats related to few of the components of biodiversity present around us. It says:

- Coral reefs provide food, storm protection, jobs, recreation and other income sources for more than 500 million people worldwide yet 70% of coral reefs are threatened or destroyed.

- 18,788 species out of 52,017 so far assessed are threatened with extinction.
- Of the world's 5,490 mammals, 78 are Extinct or Extinct in the Wild, with 188 Critically Endangered, 540 Endangered and 492 Vulnerable.
- 1,895 of the planet's 6,285 amphibians are in danger of extinction, making them the most threatened group of species known to date.

We need to realize that we obtain large number of products and services from the biodiversity present around us. Almost everything that we require on day to day basis including land, food, water, air, medicines, fibres, rubber, oil, timbers, forage, construction materials etc. are either direct products of biodiversity or these are available to us on account of the existence of biodiversity in different forms. As an example, we can discuss about water. Water is a chemical compound which is there in the environment. But, its cycling, its purification, decontamination etc. are dependent on the biodiversity. Trees and other plants play important role in bringing out the water from inside the ground and converting the same into vapour. This vapour along with the vapour formed by direct evaporation from water bodies and land comes down in the form of rain, hail, snow etc. These forms of precipitation keep the water cycle intact. Plants do not only bring out water from inside the land and convert the same into vapour. The same plants also help in percolation of water into the ground. In the absence of vegetation, the percolation is reduced and surface flow is increased. More surface flow also leads to soil erosion and nutrient loss. Together these processes lead to siltation, flood, eutrophication etc. Another contribution that vegetation makes is to reduce or remove pollutants from water. Polluted water passing through vegetated area becomes partially or fully free from common pollutants. On the other side the plants purify the atmosphere. Not only they absorb carbon dioxide and release oxygen into the atmosphere, they also absorb different types of pollutants from the atmosphere thus providing us clean air.

Trees and other types of vegetation form forests which is store house of large number of resources and also the habitat for a variety of animals which cannot survive otherwise. Hence, it is essential that conservation of biodiversity must take into account the diversity of ecosystems, diversity at species level and also at the genetic level.

Apart from the direct use values, various ecosystems perform services which result in economic gains. Obviously, the ecosystems perform their functions on account of plants, microorganisms and animals inhabiting them i.e. on account of the biodiversity present there. Efforts have been made to work out the value of these services in monitory terms. They have come to the conclusion given on next page:

A giant bamboo plant – a grass species

A tree Fern, rare in wild due to gross overuse and destruction of habitat

A variety of red rice, more nutritious and rarely seen now

A white tiger. Presently, all the white tigers in different zoos world over, are from India.

Bees help in pollination and also, produce honey

Birds following a tractor plough preying on insects coming out of soil

Ecosystem Services	*Estimated Economic Value (in US $ /ha/year)*		
	Wetland	*Forest*	*Rangeland*
Climate regulation		141	0
Disturbance regulation	4539	2	
Water regulation	15	2	3
Water supply	3800	2	
Soil formation		10	1
Erosion control		96	25
Nutrient cycling		361	
Waste treatment	4177	87	87
Pollination			25
Biological control		2	23

The values given above are per hectare. If total areas covered by different ecosystems at global level are taken into account, the values will work out to astronomical figures. These are only few of the contributions made by the ecosystems. There are many more which generally remain unaccounted. Thus, it is evident that the ecosystems and the biodiversity present there are of great value to us directly as well as indirectly and we need them for our own survival. IUCN has estimated the value of global ecosystem services. The estimates suggest that it may be anywhere between $16 to-$64 trillion, annually. Certainly, it is a huge contribution and if we lose it, we will not be able to compensate through any other means. We must realize that in the long term, the value of services lost may greatly exceed the short-term economic benefits obtained through changes in the ecosystems and associated biodiversity. We need to remember that when we modify an ecosystem to improve a service it provides, it generally results in changes with reference to other services provided by the ecosystem. For example, activities which may promise increased food production may result in reduced water availability in terms of quantity and quality for users other than the farmers. For example services like fisheries, water supply may be directly affected. Also, protection against natural hazards is likely to be affected. All these have the potential to seriously affect people's lifestyle and well-being.

Hence, it is in our own interest that the ecosystems are conserved. However, conservation should not be misunderstood as total 'No Use'. For our day to day survival, the biological and other ecosystem resources have to be used. Hence, it is essential that conservation takes into account the use of the biological resources. On the face, it seems impossible. We want to use the resources and also we want to conserve them. But, it is possible. We have to adopt the philosophy of sustainable use of biodiversity. It would mean that we have to adopt a strategy so that we may use the resources and also see to it that there is no decline of the diversity on long term basis. Only then the needs and expectations of the present generation can be met and also it will be ensured that the future generation will not suffer on account of loss of biodiversity. Let us take one example to explain this. Suppose in a forest there are one thousand plants of a particular species of medicinal value. We need to exploit this resource for our well being. We have two options. We take out all or most of the plants and later, we learn that the plant population left is not large enough to survive in long term. As a result, the total population will be lost and we will not be in a position to use the resource in future. Another possibility is that we find out the size of viable population for long term survival and regeneration of the species concerned. If it is six hundred, we must be careful to harvest only such number of plants that at least six hundred are always there in the wild. There is also the possibility that we only harvest certain parts of the plants so that it may regenerate. Quite often the same is not practiced. For example overharvesting is done or unscientific harvesting is practiced. Example can be found in case of medicinal plants or in other similar items which we obtain form our environment. Frequently, we come across examples in case of fishing that the fishermen go on reducing the diameter of the holes in their net to catch more fish. They rarely realize that by doing so they are destroying the future resource i.e. the immature and young population of fishes. Finally, the fishermen suffer on account of lower catch resulting in loss in income.

Now let us try to understand the prevalent reasons behind loss in biodiversity. Reasons are many. An important one is lack of awareness and education. Quite often people who work at the ground level are not aware of the implications. They learn only after the tragedy has occurred. An example can be cited about mangroves and coral reefs. Most of the people consider these ecosystems and organisms associated with them as not of great value. As a result they overexploit the resources and as a consequence degrade or destroy the ecosystems. Only at a later stage they realize that destruction of mangroves and coral reefs lead to fall in the total productivity of the coastal area, including fish production. We also need to understand that at times such overexploitation is on account of compulsion. Poor and marginalized families have nothing else to sustain themselves. So, they exploit all possible resources. There is one another possibility. Poor people over-exploit the resources at the behest of contractors and industrialists to whom they sell the harvest. The contractors and industry owners have no permanent stake in the sustainability of the ecosystems. Hence, they are least concerned about their degradation and destruction. If we plan to conserve and protect the biodiversity present in the country, it is essential that there is equity in use as well as conservation. It cannot be expected that those who are powerful and resourceful will use the biodiversity while the less privileged will contribute to its conservation.

Chief Seattle (Sealth) was born in 1790 and was one of the great chiefs of a federation of tribes occupying the shores of Lake Washington near the current site of Seattle. Reproduced here is selected portion of his moving reply to an offer in 1854 by the United States Government for a large area of Indian land.

He said "How can you buy or sell the sky the warmth of the land? The idea is strange to us. If we do not own the freshness of the air and the sparkle of the water, how can you buy them?

Every part of this earth is sacred to my people. Every shining pine needle, every sandy shore, every mist in the dark woods, every clearing and humming insect is holy in the memory and experience of my people. The sap which courses through the trees carries the memories of the red man. The white man's dead forget the country of their birth when they go to walk among the stars. Our dead never forget this beautiful earth, for it is the mother of the red man. We are part of the earth and it is part of us. The perfumed flowers are our sisters, the deer, the horse, the great eagle, these are our brothers. The rocky crests, the juices in the meadows, the body heat of the pony and man – all belong to the same family.

The rivers are our brothers, they quench our thirst. The rivers carry our canoes, and feed our children. If we sell you our land, you must remember, and teach your children that the rivers are our brothers, and yours, and you must henceforth give the rivers the kindness you would give any brother.

The clatter only seems to insult the ears. And what is there to life if a man cannot hear the lonely cry of the whippoor will or the arguments of the frogs around a pond at night? I am a red man and do not understand. The Indian prefers the soft sound of the wind darting over the face of a pond, and the smell of the wind itself cleaned by a midday rain, or scented with the pinion pine.

So we will consider your offer to buy our land. If we decide to accept, I will make one condition the white man must treat the beasts of this land as his brothers. I am a savage and I do not understand any other way. I have seen a thousand rotting buffaloes on the prairie, left by the white man who shot them from a passing train.

I am a savage and I do not understand how the smoking iron horse can be more important than the buffalo that we kill only to stay alive. What is man without the beasts? If all the beasts were gone, man would die from a great loneliness of spirit. For whatever happens to the beasts, soon happens to man. All things are connected.

Thus we know the earth does not belong to man, man belongs to the earth. This we know. All things are connected like the blood which unites one family. All things are connected. Whatever befalls the earth befalls the sons of the earth. Man did not weave the web of life he is merely a strand in it. Whatever he does to the web, he does to himself."

Now let us look at the scientific aspect of the need for conservation of biodiversity, with especial reference to India. So far we know very little about the rich bio-diversity of our country. We have not been able to even identify and list all the species. As far as their genetic contents, chemical composition, contents of useful chemicals and ingredients, possibilities of their use in future etc. are concerned. We are in total dark for most of them. On the other hand, regularly, we come across examples which go to prove that organisms which were earlier considered to be of no importance have been found to be of immense value. Hence, if we lose a species without discovering all its properties, and possible use, it is likely that we may lose a valuable resource which could otherwise bring benefits to the humanity. Let us take the example of a common plant found all over the country. Its botanical name is Catharanthus roseus. In Hindi it is called 'Sadaa bahaar'. It is grown in gardens and it also grows wild near roads, parks, and on unused land. Till recently this plant was not considered of any great significance. Recently, it was found that the plant produces vinblastine and vincristine. These are two alkaloids, present in the leaves of the plant. These two chemicals and vindesine and vinorelbine which are semi-synthetic derivatives of vinblastine, have the potential to inhibit division of living cells. So, they possess the potential to control cancer. Large quantity of the plant is being imported by USA and other countries for extraction of the two alkaloids. Already the chemicals are in use for control of certain types of cancer. Extensive research work is going on in various countries to find further use of the chemicals for control and cure of other types of cancer.

Another interesting example is of a common plant Phyllanthus amarus ('Bhui amla'). Few years back, Dr.B.S. Blumberg, a Nobel Laureate from USA, who had discovered Hepatitis 'B' virus, was in India and here he got a lead about the plant. This plant has been traditionally used in India for treatment of jaundice. Through his research he could establish that Phyllanthus amarus could cure Hepatitis 'B' infection as well and he could obtain two patents on Phyllanthus amarus. There was a move from Indian side to challenge the patents. But, it could not be possible as the Indian traditional literature never documented that Phyllanthus amarus could cure Hepatitis 'B', although the plant has been used in India for centuries for treatment of jaundice and other liver related disorders. A drug has been developed for improving memory from semi-aquatic herbs Bacopa monnieri and Centella asiatica. These plants have been traditionally used in India for improving memory power. Now Aamla, Kathal (Jack fruit), Sahjan (Drumstick) and Bael (Wood apple) are being cultivated here and there. Till recently these were found only in the wild and the fruits and other parts were collected from there. Still only a very small proportion of these products come from the cultivated areas. Most of the materials used as vegetable, fruit or for medicinal use come from the wild. There are many such plants which grow as part of wild biodiversity and are used as food materials or for their medicinal properties. We need to realize that at least 35000 species of plants are expected to have medicinal value.

Only about 5000 species have been studied so far in some detail for their medical applications. Thus the possibilities are immense. In this regard surveys conducted in USA are quite important. It was found that 118 of the top 150 prescription drugs were originally from living organisms. 74% were from plants, 18% from fungi, 5% from bacteria and 3% from animals. World Health Organization (WHO) has estimated that 80% of the population in the developing countries is dependent on traditional cure systems for their health care. The traditional cure system is based on materials which are derived from plants. China produces more than 40000 types of traditional plant drugs. In India too very large varieties of plants are used as medicines. A recent report says that a small red-eyed frog has the promise to cure AIDS. It has been found that a chemical present in the skin of the red-eyed tree frog, generally found in Australia, has the capacity to block infection by HIV. The chemical destroys the virus particles which result in AIDS. Scientists are working on ideas to produce lotion which may protect against HIV and AIDS. This is just an example. With further investigations relating to different plants and animals such possibilities may multiply. But the same will be possible only if we conserve the animals, plants and other organisms i.e. the biodiversity present in different parts of the world.

VALUE OF BIODIVERSITY:

The biological resources and ecosystems play important role in providing for human security and human development. By way of agriculture, fishing, forestry etc. the biodiversity provides us various items which help in building up national economies and generate employment. Products obtained from different ecosystems are many such as food, water, fodder, timber, medicines, fibres, leather, fuel etc. Also, nutrient recycling, control of drought and flood, production of soil, purification of water and air are done by the ecosystems. We do not have to pay anything for these services rendered by the ecosystems. Hence, at times we do not attach any value to these services. If we calculate the price of these services at national or regional level, the cost will be astronomical. For USA, some calculations have been done. Value of the annual crop production is estimated to be about \$ 40 billion. No doubt, the farmers work on their farms, they do plowing and sowing, apply fertilizer and irrigate the crops. But, all this cannot yield any result if the flowers are not pollinated. Large numbers of the crop species are adapted to only insect pollination. Hence, without the contribution of lowly insects the process of pollination cannot succeed and there will be no fertilization which leads to formation of fruits and seeds. But, the crops go on producing year after year because there are insects which pollinate the flowers. So, what we get from our crops is very much dependent on the insects and similar other pollinators about which we never bother. If we look in monetary terms, it is very difficult to get a precise estimate of the value of pollination done by insects and other living organisms. Estimates suggest that this activity alone represents tens of billions of dollars in ecosystem services per annum to humankind. Similarly, pests controlled by biological agents account for about \$ 100 to 200 billion. The value of biologically

fixed nitrogen is estimated to be about $ 50 billion. If we try to replace these natural agents by chemicals or synthetic processes, the cost will be totally prohibitive. In addition, we will have to run thousands of industries to manufacture the pesticides and fertilizers. What would be the impact of those industries on our environment is beyond imagination.

As noted earlier, not much work has been done to assess the value of biodiversity in monetary terms. Only isolated instances are there from few places. If we take the case of insects alone, we come to the figures which show that the insects contribute more than $57 billion. This is a conservative estimate as the estimate related to only four services provided by the insects. Nutrition provided to wildlife by insects worked out to $50 billion, pest control by way of insects preying upon other insects worked out to be $4.5 billion, pollination of crops by insects was of $3 billion value, conversion of dung into compost worked out to be $380 million. The study related to only wild insects. Contribution of commercially reared insects is additional. We know how much silk, honey etc. are produced by these insects.

There are various other instances which prove beyond doubt that biodiversity at all levels is important for our survival. An example can be cited here from the Himalayas. Apples are the main cash crop in large areas of the Hindu Kush-Himalayas. They account for about 60 to 80 percent of the total houselhold income. Over 84 hilly and mountainous districts of India, Pakistan, China, Nepal and Bhutan grow apples in about 320000 hectares. It is estimated that apple production in the region is over 2.5 million tonnes, generating income to the tune of US $ 450 million per annum. Recently, farmers from the region have been complaining of decreasing production even with improved inputs. Investigations carried out by ICIMOD (International Centre for Integrated Mountain Development), Kathmandu revealed that the root cause was failure of pollination in apple crops. It was being triggered by the disappearance of wild bees, butterflies, moths etc. There are not enough carriers for the pollen grains from one flower to another leading to failure of fruit setting. Certain corrective measures have been suggested which includes rearing of honey bees and reduced use of insecticides. Hence, if we want to have a sustained livelihood, we have to realize the contributions being made by the total biodiversity. Also, genetic resources which help in creation of new organisms and improvement of the existing ones are provided by living organisms which are part of the biodiversity.

Scientists in USA have worked out in 2007 the percentage of some of the valuable fruits, vegetables, nuts and field crops which depend on insects for pollination, particularly honeybees. The results are given-

Type of crop	*Percentage of pollination by honeybees*	*Value in billions of $*
Almonds	***100***	***2.2***
Apples	***90***	***2.1***
Blueberries (cultivated)	***90***	***0.5***
Cotton	***16***	***5.2***
Grapes	***1.0***	***3.2***
Oranges	***27***	***1.8***
Peanuts	***2.0***	***0.6***
Peaches	***48***	***0.5***
Soybeans	***5***	***19.7***
Strawberries	***2***	***1.5***

Obviously, the value in money terms must have gone up with increase in the prices of the products. Another important point is that almonds depend totally on honey bees for pollination and apples to the extent of 90%. This explains the reduction in apple production in the Hindukush Himalayas on account of reduction in insect population, as discussed above.

Experiments have clearly shown that humans cannot easily build ecosystems to support human needs. We have to remain dependent on nature for most of our needs. We have discussed pollination done by insects. With all our scientific advancements we cannot mimic insect pollination.

We quite often observe that traditionally honeybee keepers keep their boxes close to orchards and farms. The orchard managers and farmers welcome the bee keepers as they know that the bees help in production of grains, fruits, seeds etc.

By now we have discussed several aspects of benefits that we get from biodiversity. But it does not end there. Biodiversity has various other dimensions too. For example, it is extremely important for people living low technology lifestyles. They depend on land and water for a variety of products on which they sustain themselves. In the absence of such resources and products their standard of living will suffer and finally their existence may be in jeopardy. This is a very important reason why it is not easy to assign exact economic value to the biodiversity. We are normally trained to assign values to any commodity only as per the standard economic principles. For example, we assign productive use value for commodities which are systematically harvested and sold in the market. Common examples related to wild biodiversity are construction timber, fuel wood, fodder, fish, marine products, rattan, fibres, medicinal plants, honey, wax, natural perfumes, dyes, gums, resins, certain fruits, spices etc. But we need to understand that there could also be direct and consumptive values to a large number of products. These products are unlikely to appear in national or international markets. Fodder, fuel wood, certain food materials, fruits, grains, medicines, building materials, fibres etc. obtained from wild plants and animals by individuals or by the community at small scale are common examples. These commodities never reach the market. Either these are consumed locally or these are bartered. Hence, it is difficult to assign exact market value to these products. As a result most of the economic indicators and statistics either do not account for such products. At times if these are taken into account their actual value is never accounted for. These are grossly undervalued. If we do rational accounting, these products will emerge of great importance especially in poor countries and more so for the poorer sections of the society. An appropriate example is of medicinal plants, which we have discussed earlier too. WHO (World Health Organization) has estimated that in developing countries about 80 % of the population depends on medicinal plants directly or indirectly for their health related problems. WHO has estimated that In India itself we have about a million folk practitioners including midwives, bone-setters, "Vishva Vaidyas" etc. The systems of treatment practiced by these 'doctors' are dependent on medicinal plants, animal products, and minerals. Even at international level, the WHO estimates that about 30% of the world population still relies on herbal medicines. Most of the medicinal plants and also animal products are obtained from the wild i.e. their availability is directly dependent on the wild biodiversity. This is the reason that relevance of biodiversity to human health is becoming a major international political issue. Scientific evidences are building up in support of the wide ranging global health implications and biodiversity loss. Rich countries which do not have rich biodiversity are insisting that the poor countries which control most of the biodiversity on the Earth must protect the biodiversity for the entire world. One of the key health issues associated with biodiversity is that of drug discovery and the availability of medicinal resources. We have already seen earlier how medicinal plants contribute not only in direct healthcare but also in discovery of new drugs and medicines. On the other hand the poor countries insist that they cannot conserve their biodiversity for others at the cost of their people. They need resources including land to increase food production. To obtain more land these countries are destroying the forests and wild habitats. This is resulting in loss of biodiversity.

The present estimates indicate that in many communities, especially in poor countries, food materials obtained ftom wild sources account for over 40% of the total consumption. We can easily find people collecting wild flowers, fruits, seeds, nuts, berries, corms, bulbs etc. for use as food. Also, several types of insects and animals collected from wild are used as food. At times such food materials are more nutritious and wholesome and their availability saves the poor from starvation and malnutrition. We must not forget that although about 80 percent of our food supply comes from just 20 kinds of plants, humans use at least 40,000 species of plants and animals a day. Many people around the world depend on these species for their food and also shelter and clothing. Now it is evident that there is untapped potential for increasing the range of food products suitable for human consumption. But it is possible only if the high present rate of extinction can be stopped.

An owl on a tree. Wrong notions lead to killing of owls.

Different types of seeds considered a delicacy, on sale in a store at Bahrain Airport

Water chestnut a product from aquatic habitat i.e. ponds

Women collecting firewood from neighbourhood in Delhi

There are large numbers of examples which clearly indicate the value of biodiversity and the cost we have paid for ignoring the same. Here we will take two cases to illustrate the same. In 1846 there was the famous Irish Potato Blight. About one million persons were killed on account of the scarcity of potato caused by the Blight disease. Also, about one million persons were forced to migrate from Ireland on account of the crisis. The basic reason was that the farmers were growing only two varieties of potato and both were susceptible to the disease. If they were growing more varieties probably the picture could be different. Thus they paid heavily for ignoring the wide scale of biodiversity in case of potato. The other example is of rice. In 1970s rice crop was affected by Rice grassy stunt virus from Indonesia to India causing large scale loss to the crop. The challenge was serious as rice was and is very important for millions of residents of these countries. More than 6200 varieties of rice plants were tested to find resistance against the disease. Finally, one Indian variety was isolated which was resistant to the virus. That particular variety was hybridized with other varieties and the resistance was transferred to other varieties. Presently, those disease resistant varieties are grown widely. Thus the presence of a particular variety i.e. one small component of the total rice biodiversity proved savior.

The biodiversity rich areas provide avenues for social and psychological health, and also for spiritual well-being. We know that people visit forest areas, lakes, coastal areas, mountains etc. on account of these factors. They feel pleasure in these areas, mainly on account of the environment there which depends to a great extent on the biodiversity present there.

Another important aspect of biodiversity is that it provides the genetic base for continuous improvements in the fields of agriculture, animal husbandry etc. The cultivated and domesticated species and varieties need to be regularly manipulated and improved to meet the challenges of greater expectations and also to survive in constantly changing environment. Simple selection or genetic manipulation is employed to obtain desired improvements. However, it is possible only if we have the genetic base for improvement. In nature the genetic base is provided by the wild relatives of crops and domesticated animals. India is extremely rich in this resource. In this regard it is important to note that a large number of species of plants and animals found in India are endemic i.e. these are not found in other parts of the world. The present estimates indicate that more than 22,000 species of plants and animals fall under this category. It means that if these are lost in India, the whole world will lose them. To understand it in simple terms, we can take the example of the eight breeds of buffaloes found in India. They represent the entire range of genetic diversity of buffaloes on this Earth. If we lose any of these, it would mean that the whole world will lose it.

We have learnt so many scientific lessons from biodiversity present around us. Let us take few examples. In the field of communication there is no parallel to animals. They use different techniques for communication. One of them is smell. Smell is generated by chemicals and it can travel to long distances. The chemical signal, which was first deciphered, was of silkworm. The female produces a chemical in its abdominal gland. The chemical is so potent that one single molecule is sufficient to draw attention of the male. As a result males fly to reach the females from long distances. As the male nears the female, the signal becomes stronger and finally, the male too secretes a chemical. In response to the same the female accepts the male. Another example is the firefly. The flies have the capability to convert about 95% of the energy into light. This is done by converting a chemical luciferin into oxyluciferin. An enzyme, luciferase acts as catalyst for the reaction. If we compare that efficiency with our own devices, we will be falling behind drastically. Most of our energy devices have efficiency ranging only between ten to forty percent. Another interesting example is of plants which protect themselves against insect pests. The plants synthesise molecules that interfere with development of the larvae of plant eating insects. Due to these chemicals the larvae are unable to mature into adults. So, the plants get protection against possibility of large number of insects being produced. We have learnt to use similar technology to protect our products and materials from insects. For example, flavours of tea and lemon grass, mint, curry, coriander, thyme leaves etc. are used to keep insects away. It is quite likely that the primitive human being started to use leaves to cover their body based on the observations of certain insects or birds. For example, the tailor bird prepares its nest by neatly sewing leaves and other materials while there are insects which glue leaves to prepare their nests. On the other hand, there are some wasps which make paper for making their nests. They chew up plant materials and take out the fibres. The fibres are then glued using their saliva to form sheets in similar fashion as we make paper today. Certain insects use mud to build their homes. It is not impossible that primitive human learnt the same technique from insects to build the earliest homea. It is also important to know that we are not the first one on this earth to practice agriculture. Much before us the tiny ants started agriculture and they still do it.

Ants developed a sophisticated type of agriculture about fifty million years ago. There are three types of ants, which culture and eat fungi. The fungus growing ants generally cut pieces of leaves and bring them to their nest. In the field, the leaves are cut to size so that it can be carried by an ant. Once in the nest, the leaf pieces are cut into smaller pieces. After that the ants apply oral secretions to the leaves and add fragments of fungal mycelia from their garden. The ants maintain pure culture of the fungus of their choice for the purpose. The ants also manure their fungal gardens with their own excretory materials. Now, it has been discovered that when some new colony of ants is to be established, the new queen gets a tuft of fungal mycelia as dowry. Obtained from the garden of the mother, it is carried in the mandibles by the new queen. There are about 200 species of ants which are totally dependent on fungal farming. They have not learnt any other mode of living.

We must learn a lesson from the ants. They only consume the fungi and not the leaves. They know the fungi are able to regenerate while leaves have to be brought from outside which require labour. Also, suitable leaves are not always available readily.

Another aspect is that biodiversity poor areas are known to recover more slowly from shocks such as fire, drought, flood etc. Also, the biodiversity poor areas have less capability to resist invasion by alien species including those species which cause diseases. Common examples are Water hyacinth, Carrot grass (Parthenium), Lantana etc. These alien species try to occupy habitats which are originally occupied by local species. Once they establish, they become a menace to the health of ecosystems and also for human population. They reduce the productivity of ecosystems. Now, it has been experimentally proved that introduction of native species can eliminate the aliens. For example planting bamboos in forest areas effectively eliminated Lantana. Obvious reason is that the bamboos are the original inhabitants of the ecosystems. They have the ability to compete with the alien species on account of their adaptive capabilities. As discussed earlier, other advantages with high biodiversity is that such areas have better pollination, better production from forest, fisheries, and also from agriculture as well as faster removal of pollutants from the environment. Biodiversity is also known to have an important role in reducing disaster risk, and in post-disaster relief and recovery efforts. The Tsunami that hit India and various other countries few years ago proved it beyond doubt. Areas with rich mangrove and coral populations were much less affected than those where coasts were unguarded. In mountains mudslides and avalanches are less frequent in areas with high vegetation cover as compared to similar areas from where vegetation is missing.

Biodiversity also contributes towards better aesthetics, development of nature tourism and eco-tourism. It provides base for education, recreation and solitude. Biodiversity also has inspirational value. Taking all these aspects of biodiversity into account it is our duty to conserve the biodiversity present on this Earth. This kind of initiative will also provide the coming generations opportunity to enjoy the benefits of biodiversity, probably the greatest gift of nature.

Kalidas in 'Meghdoot' described the story of a Yaksha who got separated from his Yakshini. Yaksha requested the cloud to visit the Yakshini to find her well being. He described how the Yakshinis of Alkapuri dressed themselves. They held lotus in their hands and put flowers of jasmine in their hair. They used pollen of Lodhra to make their face glowing. For decorating their braids, they used Barleria, Kurabaka etc. They loved to put Siris flowers in their ears while Kadam was kept on the head like crown.

Nowhere else in the world literature, this kind of use of floral biodiversity can be found.

□□□

CHAPTER 9

Reasons for Biodiversity Loss

Nature does no wrong but retaliates to the wrong doing of mankind with greater force. *Saint Jambojee, founder of Bishnoi Sect.*

Generally when most people think of the dangers besetting the natural world, they think of the threat being faced by well known species. Declines in the numbers of charismatic animals like pandas, tigers, elephants and whales etc. as well as birds like cranes, geese, bustard, hornbill etc. have been able to draw world attention. Similarly, certain known varieties of plants of some value have drawn attention of people as their population is decreasing fast. Together these animals and plants have made even common people aware of the risk being faced by living organisms on Earth. Now it is estimated by scientists that species of living organisms have been disappearing at up to 1000 times the natural rate. More importantly, it is predicted that the rate of extinction is likely to rise further if corrective measures are not adopted soon. Based on the current trends, it is estimated that 34,000 plant and 5,200 animal species, including one in eight of the world's bird species, face extinction within short span of time. It has been argued that the present rate of extinction is sufficient to eliminate most species on the planet Earth within 100 years. One clear indication is that for thousands of years human race has been selecting and developing a vast array of domesticated plants and animals. Most of these animals and plants were important as food resource. But in recent times this treasure is shrinking as modern commercial agriculture focuses on relatively few crop varieties. Similarly, about 30% of breeds of the main farm animal species are currently at high risk of extinction as these are no more considered important. As a result their population is shrinking fast which may lead to the situation that in near future their population may not remain viable. We know that population of any species remains viable if a minimum number of individuals are there. If it was not so all animals and plants could be saved by keeping them in zoos or botanical gardens.

Generally, the loss of individual species catches our attention first. Reason is obvious. We know the species and it is likely that we know the species as we are benefitted by the species. But it is the fragmentation, degradation, and outright loss of forests, wetlands, coral reefs, and other ecosystems that poses the gravest threat to biological diversity. We know that forests are home for much of the known terrestrial biodiversity, but about 45 per cent of the Earth's original forests are gone, cleared mostly during the past century. Despite some re-growth and afforestation efforts, the world's total forests are still shrinking rapidly. This trend is particularly obvious in the tropics where biodiversity is highest. Similarly, up to 10 per cent of coral reefs, which are among the richest ecosystems, have been destroyed and one third of the remaining face collapse during the next one or two decades. Mangroves, which provide habitat to countless species, are dwindling fast. Half of the coral areas are already finished on global scale.

Atmospheric changes, such as green house effect and ozone depletion are further adding to the stress. We know that thinner ozone layer will let more ultraviolet-B radiation reach the Earth's surface where it can damage living organisms. Global warming caused by accumulation of greenhouse gases in the atmosphere is already changing habitats and the distribution of species. Scientists have warned that one-degree increase in the average global temperature can push many species over the brink. Our agriculture and food production systems will also be seriously disrupted bringing more pressure on the other ecosystems which support the wild biodiversity.

Loss of biodiversity has the capability to reduce the productivity of ecosystems, resulting in shrinkage of goods and services which we obtain from nature. It can directly destabilize the ecosystems, and also weaken their ability to deal with natural disasters such as floods, droughts, and hurricanes. The ecosystems also lose their ability to withstand human generated stresses, such as pollution and climate change. Already, we are facing huge losses on account of floods and storms which are direct or indirect consequences of deforestation. These losses will further increase on account of greenhouse effect and consequent global warming.

The reduction in biodiversity also hurts us in several other ways. Our cultural identity is deeply rooted in our biological entities. Plants and animals are symbols commonly used for flags, sculptures, and other images that define us and our societies. So often we draw inspiration from nature. We use the inspiration for our joy and for our creativity.

While loss of species has always occurred as a natural phenomenon, the pace of extinction has accelerated dramatically as a result of human activity. Ecosystems are being fragmented or eliminated, and innumerable species are in decline or are already extinct. We are creating the greatest extinction crisis since the natural disaster that wiped out the dinosaurs about 65 million years ago. These extinctions are irreversible. Considering our dependence on food crops, medicinal species and other biological resources for our survival, these extinctions may pose a threat to our own well-being and survival. We must realize that it is reckless even if not downright dangerous to keep losing our life support system. Also, it is unethical to drive other forms of life to extinction, and thereby deprive present and future generations of opportunities to utilize the resources for betterment of their life.

We need to realize the value of world's ecosystems. These ecosystems sustain the species value of which we already know and also the other millions of species value of which we not realized so far. But many of them may produce the foods and medicines of tomorrow. The answer can be found in our ability to bring our demands into line with nature's ability to produce what we need and to safely absorb the wastes and pollutants what we discard.

Changes of land use, especially conversion of natural ecosystems to cropland, is an important factor in reduction and disappearance of various types of natural ecosystems. This kind of threat to the ecosystems is the most important direct cause of biodiversity loss. So far more than fifty percent of the Earth's 14 terrestrial biomes have lost between 20% and 50% of their area on account of conversion of the land use pattern. The changes have generally involved conversion of natural ecosystem areas to agricultural areas.

Unsustainable use of ecosystems and over-exploitation of biodiversity are exerting additional pressures on biodiversity. Large number of species are used by us to fulfill our basic needs. In this regard it is important that many species are declining on account of their utilization at unsustainable levels. Another factor is that the species are being harvested in unscientific manner resulting in their decline which threatens the ecosystems from where these species are harvested. This kind of decline is widespread and can be observed world over with verifying intensity.

Climate change is becoming a bigger concern for the environment as more and more evidences are gathering in support of the rising temperature of the Earth and consequent impact on global climate. Climate change is expected to become a progressively more significant threat to biodiversity in the coming decades than it was supposed to be till few years ago. It is evident from the changes in flowering time, migration patterns of various animals and birds as well as the distribution of species worldwide. Scientists inform that in Europe the beginning of the growing season has advanced by 10 days on average during the last forty years. Changes like these may change food chains and also create mismatches within ecosystems. For example, in case of fish, birds and various other animals, the selection of timing for producing young ones is dependent on optimum food availability. Once the time for optimum food availability in the ecosystems is altered, the dependent species will suffer till they adopt the new timing of food availability. It may take time and till that time the population may shrink in lieu of expanding or remaining at the same level.

Introduction of alien species in ecosystems brings additional threat to the ecosystems. Plants, animals and micro-organisms are at times transported deliberately and introduced in the ecosystems. Also, these are accidentally introduced into various ecosystems outside their natural geographical ranges. On the one hand alien species try to compete with the native species for food. In addition, the aliens can spread diseases and lead to genetic changes on account of inter-breeding with the native species or populations. So far more than 530 alien species have been identified in 57 countries. These species have been found to have adverse impact on biodiversity. These are the cases for which data were collated. The average was found to be 50 species for one country and the range was nine to 200 for one country. With time information about the number of these species may grow on account of more intense research. Also, with growing interaction between various countries number of alien species migrating and establishing at other places and in different ecosystems may increase.

For surface water bodies accumulation of phosphorus and nitrogen are creating serious hazards. These nutrients reach to the water bodies on account of use of excess fertilizers on farmlands, and also from sewage and other effluents. These nutrients help algae to grow in the water. The algae themselves can prove toxic becoming health hazard. However in terms of biodiversity more damage is caused due to decomposition dead algal biomass. Decomposition consumes oxygen leading to anoxic conditions in the water bodies. Due to lack of oxygen in water plants and animals normally found in water are killed resulting in "dead zones". This term is used particularly for large areas devoid of normal plants and animals in the seas and oceans. Studies show that the number of such dead zones in different seas and oceans increased from 149 in 2003 to over 200 in 2006. Expected increase in release of pollutants and nutrients from urban and agricultural sources combined with growing development in coastal areas and more intense agriculture may result increase in the number of dead zones in future. Disposal of plastic wastes into the oceans is an additional reason for degradation of the ocean environment leading to further loss in biodiversity. Recently an ocean conservationist group has claimed that there is approximately 315 billion pounds (about 120 billion kg) of plastic in the oceans. We know that plastic is practically non-biodegradable and stays in the environment for very long time. During its stay in the environment it can harm living organisms leading to their death which in the long run may lead to disappearance of species from the oceans.

Thus, various reasons can be assigned to the loss of biodiversity. Important among these are:

Habitat loss,

Encroachment and degradation of natural ecosystems,

Unscientific and unsustainable exploitation of natural resources,

Hunting of wild species,

Unscientific methods of fishing and over fishing,

Collection of wild species for various reasons,

Introduction of exotic species which eliminate the naturally growing species, and

Pollution,

Also, disasters and accidents lead to loss in wild biodiversity.

A recently added cause is the change in climate on global and regional levels. We discussed it earlier too. Our own activities are adding certain gases in the atmosphere and their natural concentrations are increasing at unprecedented rate. Common examples are carbon dioxide, methane, CFCs (Chloro fluoro carbons) etc. Carbon dioxide is increasing in the atmosphere on account of high rate of burning of fossil fuels, deforestation and degradation of aquatic habitats and death of organisms. Methane is increasing in the atmosphere due to use of fossil fuels, from aquatic habitats on account of anoxic conditions and discharge of methane with intestinal gases of certain types of animals. As far as CFCs are concerned, concentrations of these chemicals are increasing in atmosphere due to industrial and historical use of these chemicals in certain household appliances.

Habitat destruction leads to reduction in areas occupied by forests, grasslands, freshwater bodies, marine ecosystems etc. Degradation of these ecosystems leads to loss in productivity of these ecosystems. Poaching and hunting, combined with habitat destruction have threatened the existence of several species of animals and birds. Here we can cite the example of Lesser florican. This bird is a member of the Bustard family. These birds prefer to walk than fly. To facilitate the same, they have long legs. Till recently, these beautiful birds could be seen in large numbers in the grasslands of the entire Indian subcontinent. At present these birds are threatened due to fast conversion of grasslands into agricultural areas. Some contribution is being made by their large size and easy prey to hunting for table purposes. Similarly, over-utilization and over- harvesting have resulted in depletion of resources like medicinal plants, timber species, fishes, marine flora and fauna etc.

Another important cause for loss of biodiversity in our own country has been the developmental model, which we adopted after Independence. We took up various developmental activities without paying attention to environment. Also, interdepartmental coordination was weak. As a result large areas with natural ecosystems were diverted for mining, industry, urbanization, infrastructure development etc. Such areas included even those which were supporting rich biodiversity. A parallel development was state ownership replacing the common property rights. Where state ownership was not feasible, private individual rights were introduced. This change resulted in uncontrolled harvesting of natural resources. People consider the resources as belonging to the government. They go on utilizing the same unconcerned of long term to implications. Also, corruption in various government departments has caused immense loss to natural resources and ecosystems. People pay heavy bribe to obtain rights for exploitation, harvest and use. Once they pay the bribe they are allowed to exploit the resources in uncontrolled and unrestricted manner. Also, they are not made accountable for degradation of the environment and associated ecosystems. We can easily large numbers of such examples in mining areas, exploitation of forest resources, coastal zone resources etc. Lack of awareness and education can also result in loss of biodiversity. For small gains people have been destroying natural habitats, including sacred groves, sacred ponds etc. Similarly, some of the old traditions have been forgotten leading to loss in biodiversity. Common examples are disinterest towards mixed cultivation, growing of traditional varieties of crops and other plants, maintenance of certain parts of rivers as no fishing areas, restrictions on fishing during spawning season, allowing birds and other animals to live in habitations and feeding them when required.

A signage near railway track, to protect elephants crossing the track

Signage on a highway passing through a National Park. Wild animals crossing the road are always under threat.

Original Ashoka's Edict on stone with guidelines to protect forests and wildlife

A signage put near the original Ashoka's edict – the earliest move by a king to protect the biodiversity

People collect honey for use as food and medicine. Honey bees are in danger on account of excessive application of pesticides.

A mangrove area in Andaman suffering degradation as the area is being used for ship repair

A shop selling different types of fishes and prawns – biodiversity in daily life

We know that Green Revolution brought large number of benefits to the country. However, one aberration, which is an outcome of the revolution, has harmed the environment and biodiversity drastically. It is the excessive use of pesticides. Application of excessive pesticides have adverse impacts on different components of the environment. Quite obvious is the telling impact on bird population. Sometime back, the book Rachel Carson's 'Silent Spring' did help in bringing this issue under focus. DDT was banned in most of the developed world after the publication of the book. Later, other pesticides were also banned on account of the lessons from DDT. But certain countries including India have provisions for use of the banned pesticides for specific purposes. However, their availability in the market makes it impossible to make their use totally fool proof. These are being used regularly in agriculture sector too leading to contamination of soil, water and even food products. Soil and water contamination leads to death of different species of organisms bringing pressure on biodiversity. Same is the case with plants which are not of direct use. Quite often we destroy them without being aware of their real value. Another development which is causing threat to the natural biodiversity of the country is that increasingly larger areas are coming under intensive agriculture, monoculture etc. leading to loss of traditional varieties and related biodiversity. In case of livestock too we are adopting the same strategy. Slowly, we are eliminating our traditional varieties by opting to rear only selected varieties on account of higher productivity. But such varieties have less resistance to diseases and climatic aberrations prevalent in our country. If in future we like to switch back to the traditional varieties we may not have the resource base to do so.

At this point it is essential that we address certain myths about degradation of environment as these are closely associated with loss of biodiversity. The first myth is that most environmental degradation is caused by the poor. Now, it has been established beyond doubt that most of the environmental degradation is caused by non-poor on account of their production and consumption levels. The difference is much more visible in case of industrialized countries. In underdeveloped and developing countries as well the same trend continues. No doubt, under certain circumstances poor have been found to be responsible for degradation of environment. But, in most such cases, it has been established that they did so as they had no other option. For example, when poor section of the society is forced to live without adequate water supply and without adequate sanitation facilities, they use open areas for defecation and indulge in damaging water lines for extracting water. Similarly, when they are forced to live without adequate supply of affordable fuel, they indulge in chopping of branches or de-barking of trees for use as fuel. Another myth is that population growth leads to environmental degradation. It is not always so. It happens so because investment in resources like soil, water etc. are not enhanced with growth in population. As a result, population growth brings more pressure on the environment leading to its degradation. There are examples from Kenya where, even with increasing population pressures, the farmers could manage semiarid, degraded, unproductive areas in a way that those areas got rehabilitated and became profitable. The third myth is that the poor do not have the capacity to invest in environmental improvement. In this case too it has been proved that if incentives are available, the poor are more interested in investing in environmental improvements. They can mobilize more resources in the form of labour than the rich section of the society. In different parts of our own country, various water harvesting schemes have proved this point beyond doubt. When the poor were assured of their due share in the ensuing benefit, they contributed much more than the well to do. The fourth myth is that poor people do not have the technical knowledge for management of the environment. This too has been proved wrong. Poor people have enormous store of knowledge which can help in sustainable management of resources leading to conservation of biodiversity. Common examples are sound farm practices, use of medicinal plants, better utilization of local resources for food and nutrition, efficient harvesting and utilization of water resources etc. Thus it will be advisable if poor are given due importance and they are not alienated and isolated by the influential sections of the society.

□□□

CHAPTER 10

Saving Biodiversity—the Indian Context

Sacred Groves:

Very little has been published regarding sacred groves in India, but they are, or rather were, very numerous......these......as a rule, are not touched by the axe, except when wood is wanted for the repair of religious buildings.

D. Brandis (1897) First Inspector General of Forests in India.*

Indian society has a large number of traditions which can be traced back to antiquity. Many of the traditions are associated with living organisms. One of the traditions is to consider living organisms as sacred. In fact several types of living organisms are considered sacred to the extent that these are given the status of gods and goddesses. Cow is considered sacred all over India, certain varieties of monkeys are considered sacred, Tulsi plant is sacred and there are trees like Banyan, Peepal, Bael etc., which are considered sacred. Tiger and certain snakes are given the status of gods in certain parts of the country. It is said that this kind of reverence is because Indians as a community consider that nature is supreme. Probably it is so because it is the nature which provides sustenance to the human beings. This reverence is evident in the worship of Sun, Rivers, Tiger, Cow, plants, trees and even Snakes. Certainly there will be differences of opinion on this issue. But this kind of reverence is quite beneficial to the living organisms as it ensures protection for them. This attitude and reverence do not remain same for different regions and communities. Depending on the tradition and belief the list changes from one place to another and from one community to another.

An extension of this concept is that there are identified areas of forests which are considered sacred. All forms of life existing in those areas are given full protection. The forest patches and protected areas are generally called 'sacred groves' although the exact name varies from region to region. For example, in Maharashtra these groves are called *Devari*, in Jharkhand the name is *Sarnas*, in Madhya Pradesh these groves are known as *Dev*, in Karnataka the name is *Sidharavana*, in Rajasthan these are called *Orance* while in Tamil Nadu these groves are called *Sarppakavu* and in Kerala *Kav*.

---

* *Now, the designation is changed to Director General of Forests.*

One distinct feature associated with the sacred groves, by whatever name we may call them, is that these are associated with some deity. The deities can be seen in the groves in the form of stone pieces smeared with vermillion or red paint. Now the red colour is only symbolic representing blood. It signifies the blood of the victim of sacrifice. In the remote past, the victims of sacrifice were humans. This is the reason that even today at some such groves human sacrifice is offered, although only in symbolic way. Small wound is inflicted and blood is smeared on the deity. Another important feature is that the deities are kept in the open under the sky. Sheds are generally not erected over the deities. It is believed that the deities do not like to be covered. Another important feature of all such deities is that these are considered to be feminine and extremely fierce. Also, there is strong belief that these deities can bring bad luck if anyone dares to go against the dictat of the deity. Invariably, the dictat includes one clause that nothing can be removed from the sacred groves, not even a dead tree. Occasionally, certain concessions are there. For example, removal of certain plant parts for use as medicine or for religious purposes and removal of dead leaves etc., for use as fuel are permitted. Still, nothing can be done which may put the existence of living plants, animals or birds in jeopardy. This is the reason that we find that patches of ancient forests in their original form have survived as almost all over the country. These patches remained unharmed as these were parts of certain sacred groves. Quite often it can be seen that the entire area is devastated except patch which is associated with some sacred grove.

From conservation point of view the sacred groves are extremely important. As indicated above quite often these are the last patches of vegetation left in their original shape providing habitat for the plant and animal species natural to the area. These vegetation patches with associated life forms provide good example of in-situ conservation. In case of large sacred groves the distinct micro-climatic conditions associated with the flora and fauna of the area get conserved. Hence, these areas can be important resource for scientific investigation and they can also provide resources for future improvement of the related organisms, especially plants from which some food material is obtained. In certain cases sacred groves have provided habitats to endemic animals and plants. If these patches had not survived, the plants and animals endemic to the region could have vanished. Also, we come across examples where certain practical considerations were involved in declaring a grove as sacred. For example, the sacred grove of the 'Seven Sisters' near Tunbad in the Kolaba district of Konkan has a leguminous species *Entada phaseoloides*, which is a climber plant. Bark from this plant is useful in curing snake bites in case of cattle. This is the reason that people from far off places come to the grove just to obtain a piece of the bark of the climber plant.

It may be a surprise for most of us that right inside the IIT campus at Chennai, there is a sacred grove. It is named Sri Durga Peeliamman sacred grove as the deity there is Durga Peeliamman. The grove is spread over about 10 acres. It is customary to hold annual festivals in the grove for the deity and large number devotees visit the grove on those occasions. There is a tank as well close to the

grove. The grove has a rich flora including trees, shrubs and herbs. Also, there are spotted deers and black bucks in the grove. The IIT administration is making effort to protect the grove. Still, it is facing threat on account of garbage dumping, collection of fuel during festivals when devotees in large number congregate at the spot.

Eco News, April-June 2004

We also come across sacred groves which are associated with water deities. Such groves are always associated with some natural stream receiving water from perennial springs. These streams remain active even when other sources of water in the area dry up after the rainy season is over. Important reason is that the forests and vegetations from the surrounding areas have vanished while the sacred groves keep their own streams flowing. Such streams prove to be a boon for the inhabitants of the area. People receive much needed water for daily use. One such stream is present in the Sanjay Gandhi national Park near Mumbai. Tribals living in the area get water from there. Thus, quite often these sacred groves serve dual purpose. On the one hand, these patches are the repository of the natural flora and fauna of the area. On the other hand, these patches provide water.

There are several of examples where it was reported that certain plant species had vanished from an area. Later, it was found that this was true for the entire locality except few sacred groves existing in the area. If the sacred groves were not there, probably the species could have vanished completely denying the future generations of a possible resource, which may prove useful to any extent.

It is not difficult to conclude that these groves are important for us and the coming generations. We will lose not only a tradition but also the biodiversity which is present in these isolated patches of natural vegetation kept intact on account of the reverence and belief of the common people. But, a turning point is already visible. Materialism and economic considerations have started over-riding the reverence and belief of the people who control or own the sacred groves. The same sacred groves which were considered totally safe till recently are now being vandalized and even wiped out. To circumvent the possibilities of receiving the wrath of the deities associated with the sacred groves, people perform some special 'pujas' or make some offerings to the deities. If this culture spreads, it would be difficult for the sacred groves to survive for long. Another possibility is that people are made aware of the value of the surviving groves, especially with reference to biodiversity, so that they come forward to protect and conserve them. Also, the government agencies and other organizations can come forward to provide monetary assistance to individuals or society owning the sacred groves to keep them intact. For example, financial assistance is available for botanical gardens which conserve only plants and that too ex-situ. Sacred groves play more important role as these areas conserve the plants as well as animals and birds *in-situ* condition.

Before he went to school he could read the bark of trees, leaf veins, seashell convolutions, footprints and the touch of fingers;
Now he goes to school, and he can only read words.

Jennifer Fowley

Similar to the sacred groves there are ponds and small lakes which are considered sacred. Mostly, these are associated with some temple or 'Dargaah' (Mausoleum of Muslim saint) or Gurudwara etc. People try to keep those water bodies clean and also do not remove fish etc from them. In Sikkim and adjoining areas almost all the gompas (monasteries and other religious institutions) have sacred areas around their institutions. These are in the form of sacred forests, sacred lakes, sacred spaces etc. People consider those areas as holy and hence those areas remain protected. Protection so provided to forests, groves and water bodies etc. them the living organisms present there. The entire ecosystem, small or big remains protected. As a result the biodiversity present there also gets protection as the entire ecosystem, howsoever small it may be, is protected.

We have already lost large tracts of forests, a good number of wetlands, large areas of grasslands, mangroves, coral reefs etc. Simultaneously, large numbers of wild animals and plants have either become extinct or they are in the list of threatened species. A well known example is of the Cheetah. Indian Cheetah is totally extinct in the wild. Last 3 cheetahs were killed in 1947 and the species It disappeared from wild. Large scale hunting was the most important factor. We know that loss of habitat and erosion of migration corridors for larger animals has resulted in their number coming down and also in day to day animal human conflicts. Quite often we come across instances where tigers and leopards enter habitations and attack domestic animals and also humans. We generally blame the animals. But, the reason is never that the animals prefer confrontation with human beings. We need to understand that wild animals are very shy of human beings. These animals are never interested in confronting humans. But the animals are forced to enter human habitations on account of shrinkage of wild areas. Shrinkage of wild areas means loss of habitat as well as reduction in the population of prey species. Also day to day human interference in the remaining wild areas compels the animals to shed their shy nature. Once they reach that stage it becomes easy for them to confront humans.

It is quite common to come across instances of wild elephants invading agricultural areas and human settlements. But the fault is ours. Elephants require very large areas of forest for healthy lifestyle as they are herbivores. They also require migration corridors. Due to shrinkage of wild areas and disturbances in the migration corridors, the elephants get physically and emotionally disturbed. This results in human-elephant conflicts. To save their crop and properties people come out to face the wild elephants. At times humans are injured and also killed during the confrontation. But most of the time the animal is at the receiving end. In October 2010 a baby elephant strayed into fields in Assam. It was mercilessly tortured and finally killed. The incident was indicative of the deep hatred that people carry for the innocent animals. They feel that the animals enter their territory and create problems although the fact is that the animals are forced to come out of the wild and enter human settlements. The animals are forced to do so as the forest areas are shrinking fast.

Forests in the country serve as the largest ecosystems in terms of resources and also in defining the weather and climatic conditions. As noted earlier, during the second part of twentieth century the forest area in the country kept in shrinking. The same could hamper the total environmental balance as well as economic development. Hence, from time to time various initiatives and programmes were introduced in the country to protect the existing forests and to increase the forest cover in the country. In this regard we need to discuss about an initiative which was started in 1980s by few forest officials for sustainable use of forest resources along with regeneration. In course of time the initiative turned into a large scale programme called Joint Forest Management (JFM). Now, all the states have adopted the JFM programme. JFM involves voluntary agencies and village communities in the process of regeneration of degraded forest. Joint Forest Management Committees (JFMCs) have been formed at village level. The JFMCs are now managing more than 220 lakh ha of forest areas. JFMCs are given full rights over Non-Timber Forest Produce, except few items like Tendu leaves, Cashew, Sal seeds. During the last eighteen years of its implementation JFM has proved to be a highly successful programme in the field of forest management. Parallel to JFM and to complement it, a new scheme of National Afforestation was started in 2002-2003.

The Ministry of Environment and Forests constituted a National Afforestation and Eco-development Board in 1992. The Board is engaged in activities related to regeneration of degraded forest areas and lands adjoining forest areas, Protected Areas including Wildlife Sanctuaries, National Parks and ecologically fragile areas such as Aravallis, Eastern Ghats and Western Himalayas. Identified areas are declared as Ecologically Sensitive Areas by the Ministry of Environment and Forests. Such areas have restrictions related to developmental activities which have detrimental effects on the environment. Those areas are also provided facilities for restoration of denuded areas, management of catchment areas and watershed etc. so that developmental activities may progress in properly planned manner. Under this scheme Aravalli Range (Haryana and Rajasthan), Dahanu Taluka (Maharashtra), Doon Valley (Uttarakhand), Murud-Janjira area (Maharashtra) have been notified. Also, No Development Zones have been notified around Mahabaleshwar, Matheran and Panchgani (Maharashtra) and around Numaligarh Oil Refinery in Assam. For the protection and conservation of flora and fauna in the coastal areas there is the Coastal Regulation Zone (CRZ) Notification under Environment Protection Act. This Notification prohibits certain activities which may prove detrimental to the environment in the Coastal Regulation

Zone. The Zone includes up to 500 m from the high tide line of seas, backwater, bays, creeks, estuaries and rivers. Presently, there are thirty two types of developmental activities in various sectors like industry, infrastructure, mining, nuclear power, river valley projects and thermal power generation which require Environmental Impact Assessment (EIA) for obtaining clearance from environmental angel before the projects are implemented. EIA always has a strong component on biodiversity issues. The purpose is that implementation of the projects must not affect the biodiversity component in the area and mitigation measures may be adopted in advance for minor disturbances in flora, fauna and other biodiversity components. For river valley projects special emphasis is laid on aquatic and terrestrial wildlife and time bound management plans are essential to be implemented in advance to take care of possible adverse impacts. As we have learnt earlier desertification is an important threat to the biodiversity. To combat desertification a twenty year National Action Programme to Combat Desertification has been prepared by the government. The Programme will involve the local communities in effective manner in the process of implementation of various initiatives.

In case of plants, over exploitation may lead to their elimination. The plants cannot migrate. No doubt seeds do reach new areas. But there is little possibility that the plants will survive there on account of differences in the environment. Even if the plants establish in new environment, the population size may not be large enough to become viable. Similarly, the remaining population in the original habitat may not be viable in long term on account of reduced population size. We know that for any population to survive successfully a minimum size of the population is essential.

Once instances of overexploitation of important plants came to light, it became essential to take action to conserve and strengthen the plant biodiversity which we have inherited. But, we have to realize that conservation does not mean simply preserving the plants, animals and other organisms which constitute the biodiversity. Conservation must take into consideration the intra-specific (within the species) and inter-specific (between different species) diversity that exists in nature. Hence, if sample populations are preserved outside the natural habitats, the effort will be of little use. On the other hand, if we try to conserve all such habitats which are known to have high biodiversity, it may not be a viable proposition. People living in those areas and utilizing the resources present there are bound to raise objections as they may have to vacate the area or restrict their activities.

At this point it is important to understand that declaring large areas as protected renders them exclusionary. The same may yield conservation benefits for the outsiders including the international community. But, it is disadvantageous to the local communities whose access to available resources is restricted. On the other hand, if local communities are involved in conservation efforts, they will be interested in maintaining and enhancing the biodiversity as it helps them directly and indirectly. Now, it is clearly understood that natural resource degradation and loss of biodiversity affect the poor much more than those who are better off. It is so as the poor do not have the capacity to purchase all the

A sacred forest, which is protected

A sacred pond in Ladakh. People revere these ponds.

Marine biodiversity supports a large chunk of population all over the world. However, overfishing needs to be avoided for long term benefits.

Haldi or turmeric an important ingredient in Indian kitchens and medicines

Two varieties of tree seeds with wings. The wings help their dispersion but there is no guarantee that the seedlings will survive in their new habitat.

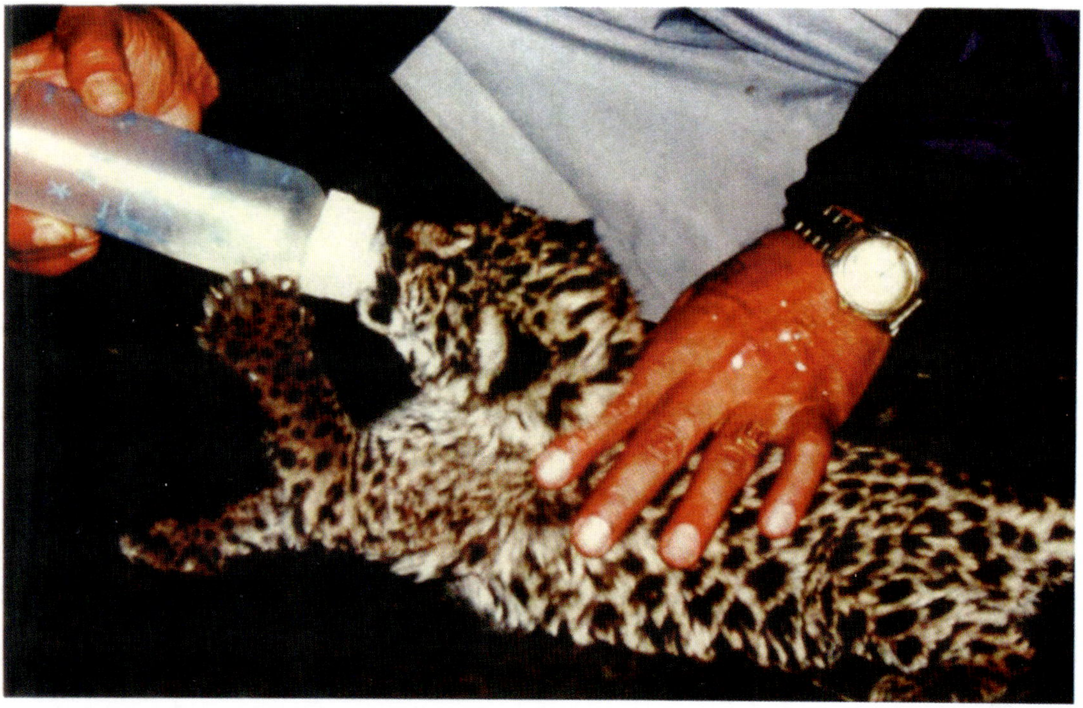

A jaguar cub being nursed in a zoo. Zoos play an important role in protecting biodiversity though they cannot substitute natural habitats.

A Hornbill on a window in the house of the author in New Delhi–a rare sight

resources from the market, even if it is available. In several communities world over it has been recorded that children having growth abnormalities caused by poor nutrition, were encountered more in communities living in areas which had suffered high level of soil degradation and loss of biodiversity. Utilization of resources is not the only reason to protect the biodiversity. Occasionally, local communities are interested in protecting the biodiversity of their area for religious or cultural reasons. This has been discussed in detail in the section dealing with "Sacred Groves".

Hence, the only alternative available is that conservation efforts should go parallel with sustainable use of the natural resources. Taking the same as goal, certain specific actions are already underway. One example is that special status has been assigned to designated areas rich in bio-diversity. Declaring specified areas as National Parks, Wildlife Sanctuaries, Biosphere Reserves or Ecologically Sensitive Areas are examples. This strategy has been found to be successful to a great extent. But, this strategy has its own limitations. As explained earlier, only limited areas can be brought under the purview of protected areas network like National Parks, Sanctuaries etc. At present, we have 100 National Parks and 514 Wildlife Sanctuaries, forty three Conservation Reserves and thirteen Community Reserves in the country covering several million ha area. Another initiative was the Project Tiger, which was launched in 1973 when the tiger population in the country had come down to as low as about 1800. The Project started with only nine Tiger Reserves. Presently, there are 38 Tiger Reserves covering more than 38600 sq. km. With the aim to provide protection to elephants Project Elephant was launched in 1992. Twenty six Elephant Reserves were notified by the middle of 2010 covering about 60,000 sq. km. area. Six more Reserves were approved in principle. Himalayas in the northern part of India supports a population of about 200 to 600 Snow leopards. In 2009 January a Project Snow Leopard was launched by the Central Government for the conservation of the habitat of the Snow leopard and the leopard itself. Similarly, there are special initiatives to protect Gharial (a crocodile), Indian Rhinoceros, Hangul or Kashmir stag, The Great Indian Bustard, vultures, Indian Sarus Crane etc. Among plants there are identified programmes for conservation of Rhododendron, Orchids and Citrus. Mangroves are being planted in areas where they can survive to compensate for the loss in the past. Mass propagation of Pitcher plants for reintroduction in their natural habitats is continuing. Also, large animals are being introduced or reintroduced in areas which are suitable for them. For example tigers have been reintroduced in Sariska Wildlife Sanctuary to compensate for their extermination on account of poaching. Similarly, rhinoceros are being relocated to Manas from Kaziranga to expand their distribution. There is proposal to introduce lion, in new areas from Gir to ensure their better survival in future. There is one another type of initiative called Biosphere Reserve. These are large areas representing a particular biogeographic zone. Fifteen such reserves have been notified. The Biospheres have been divided into core, buffer and transition area. Biosphere Reserves emphasize active participation of local communities in management of resources. With the aim to conserve and encourage sustainable utilization of medicinal plants Medicinal Plants Conservation Areas (MPCAs) have been identified in various parts of the country. More than fifty MPCAs have been covering more than 11,000 ha area have been demarcated in various states. The MPCAs are contributing substantially in in-situ and ex-situ conservation of medicinal plants.

Different types of protected areas network has proved extremely successful in protecting the biodiversity present there. However, it is not possible to widen their scope beyond a limit. It may result in conflict as declaration of specific areas as 'protected', automatically imposes various types of restrictions on the use of these areas and the resources present there. For the growing population of the country and to carry forward the developmental activities we need to utilize efficiently our environmental resources, including land. Recently, several instances of conflicts have come to the fore. Coal mining is one example. Most of the coal reserves in the country are located in the forest areas. Coal mining will lead to destruction of forests. Environmentalists are of the view that mining activities should not be allowed those areas. On the other hand those who are desirous of using coal are insisting on removing the restrictions. Another example is of the proposed airport near Mumbai. The area has mangrove vegetation. Environmentalists are insisting that the airport cannot be developed at the cost of mangroves. Those who are in support of the airport are arguing that airport is more important and even if some mangrove areas are sacrificed, the proposal must go ahead. We expect the concerned Ministries will take adequate care while arriving at some decision. Similar is the case with certain industries located in areas which are environmentally sensitive. Obviously the industries are threat to the environment and the associated biodiversity. The industries always assure that the environment will remain unaffected. But the past history does not support this kind of assurance. Also, there are chances of accidents which can cause large scale environmental damage.

Taking these and other similar factors into account, for managing and conserving the biodiversity of the country as a whole we have to have a clear strategy. Neither utilization of the resources nor conservation of biodiversity can be compromised i.e. we use the resources while conserving the biodiversity present in those areas. Obviously, this will involve some sacrifice on the part of the people who control such areas and who have the right to use the resources available there. They may have to restrict or at least modify their use pattern. On the face, it may look difficult. But it is not so. We have numerous examples from our past. Allowing wild animals, birds etc. to stay close to our settlements, providing them protection and sustenance, leaving aside certain areas as sacred groves, cultivating traditional varieties and species without giving too much importance to the possible higher yield from the newly developed varieties, abstaining from harvest of plants and fishes from identified areas on account of sanctity and reverence attached to those areas have been our age old tradition. These practices have been helping in conservation of the biodiversity present in the country in big way. We might not have been aware of these initiatives as these efforts were never undertaken in the name of conservation of biodiversity. Such traditions have been continuing as part of religion or social ritual. An example, which is cited frequently is of Bishnoi community in Rajasthan and adjoining areas. They do not cut green trees or kill animals. That is the reason that wild animals can be found roaming freely in areas dominated by the community. Also, the areas dominated by Bishnoi community are always green.

No doubt, humans have generally played the role of destruction agents as far biodiversity is concerned. But, at times they have promoted biodiversity through domestication. The oldest example is the dog. Breeds of dogs ranging from the tiny Pomeranians to the large sized Saint Bernards are the result of human manipulation.

Examples from our own subcontinent are the yak and mithun which are allied to cattle. These were domesticated in the Himalayas. A more commonly encountered example is the domestic chicken, now so commonly found everywhere. They have emerged from the North Indian red jungle fowl. Another important example is the mango. Its natural habitat is the wet forests of the Indian subcontinent. Through human interference, the distribution range of mango has extended to most of the regions of the country. It is also cultivated extensively almost all over the country and in other countries of the subcontinent. Net result is that the genetic diversity of mango has been enhanced beyond expectations. There are possibilities that also rice and water buffalo were brought under domestication in India.

There is a disturbing trend visible. With passage of time and growing pace of development and materialism, these traditions are losing their impact. Identified areas and species or varieties of plants and animals which were traditionally given protection, are unable to retain their status. An example can be cited here of the peacocks. Traditionally, peacocks have been provided protection in the country. Also, being the National Bird, it attracts special legal status. But, recently, large numbers of instances of peacocks being killed through poisoning have come to light. Obvious reason is that the farmers consider them their enemy on account of the little damage they cause to the crops. But the farmers do not realize the positive contributions made by these birds by way of controlling insects and other pests or adding charm and beauty to the surrounding. Small loss by way of reduced crop production outweighs the traditional sentiments and the legal obligations. Similarly, if we take the example of certain insects, butterflies etc., we rarely realize their contributions in pollination, decomposition of wastes and in adding beauty to the environment. While using insecticides, we rarely bother if butterflies, honey bees and other useful insects are killed. We need to be careful and adopt alternative methods to control pests. Crop rotation, biological control of pests, growing of traditional varieties which are pest resistant are few possibilities which can replace conventional chemical methods. Traditionally fishermen used to abstain from fishing for certain period every year. That period coincided with the egg laying and reproduction period of fishes. However, in recent time such traditions are becoming weak. Another initiative prevalent in the country was that of maintaining a minimum size of holes in the fishing nets. The same permitted young fish to escape unhurt. Now the fishermen are reducing the size of holes in the nets to catch more. As a result the young ones are caught and killed. Also, other animals get trapped and die. At times people kill animals and birds on account of superstition. An interesting example is of owls. During the period between Durga Puja and Diwali various types of Tantrik rituals are performed in different parts of the country. Owls and owlets are sacrificed during those rituals by the tantriks. Conservation experts are of the view that hundreds of these birds are sacrificed every year. In 2010 more than two dozen owls were recovered in Etawah, a small town of UP. How many could not be recovered and could have reached to Delhi, Mumbai, Kolkata etc. is not known. These birds are found in areas around Chambal. From there these are captured and taken to various destinations for tantric rituals. At the end the birds are going to vanish if sufficient protection is not provided and poachers do not stop capturing them for money.

Jim Corbett, the famous hunter-naturalist, was convinced half a century ago that tigers would be gone within a decade. He was obviously too pessimistic; the tigers have accompanied us into the new millennium. One may then ask: will they last the twenty first century? I think that there is an excellent chance that they will. After all, we have drastically cut down on the rate of loss of tiger's forest habitat in many parts of the country. I suspect that within the next two decades deforestation will be brought completely under check. This has kept at a moderate level the tiger-human conflict over killing of cattle. This ought to disappear in another two decades as we put in place more effective institutions of participatory management of forests and wildlife. The really serious threat now is poaching, fuelled by the demand for tiger pelt, bone and penis, and that too is partly under control.

Prof. Madhav Gadgil: in Whetstone Chatterbox, September 2001.

Ex Situ Conservation Measures: *In situ* conservation measures are quite important for protecting the biodiversity. However, at times in situ conservation measures are not possible. For such cases *ex situ* conservation measures may prove useful. Taking the same into account a number of measures are already under implementation in the country. Various botanical and zoological gardens are example of the same. The history of botanical gardens in the country dates back to more than two centuries. Large numbers of such gardens were established in different cities, towns and educational institutions. The Indian Botanical garden at Kolkata was started in 1787.Presently, it occupies 110 ha area and supports about 2,500 species of plants from different parts of the country and outside. Presently, there are 33 botanical gardens managed by various government agencies and same number of gardens managed by different universities in the country. For future there is an ambitious plan to have at least one botanical garden in each district. A huge botanical garden with the name Botanical Garden of Indian Republic has been set up in NOIDA near Delhi. It is spread in an area of about 200 acres. The Garden will focus on conservation of indigenous plants, especially threatened, rare and endangered species.

A bunch of Starfish in a pit. Occasionally, these have to be killed to protect the corals.

Crocodile farm in Andaman, an initiative for protecting threatened species

A plaque in Kuala Lumpur. It shows a tree which was to be felled to build a TV Tower, but was protected by shifting the tower.

Entry to Mount Harriet National Park in Andaman. National Parks act as safe haven for wildlife and the entire ecosystems.

Botanical Gardens play an important role in conservation of biodiversity.

First zoo in the country was started in 1854. The zoo was privately owned. First government owned zoo was established in Chennai. Presently, it is estimated that there are about 300 zoos, animal parks and aquaria in the country. Central Zoo Authority established by the Ministry of Environment and Forests provides financial and technical assistance to the zoos. It also undertakes planned breeding of endangered species so that their population may grow. Under suitable conditions the captive bred animals are introduced in the wild.

A number of gene banks have been established in the country for ex situ conservation of animals, plants, fish and microorganisms. The National Gene Bank at National Bureau of Plant Genetic Resources stores seeds of crop plants. There are more than 250,000 types of seeds preserved in the facility. National Bureau of Animal Genetic Resources was started at Karnal in Haryana in 1984. This facility with other institutes and laboratories conserves germplasm of various animals of economic importance. National Bureau of Fish Genetic Resources works on ex situ conservation methods for fish genetic resources of the country. National Bureau of Agriculturally Important Microorganisms specializes in biodiversity of microbes, particularly soil borne fungi which cause diseases. The Bureau also collects and preserves bacteria, yeasts, Actinomycetes and other types of fungi. Also, three National Gene Banks for medicinal plants have been established in different places. These banks conserve species of plants which are known for their medicinal properties and are rare, threatened or endangered. A special programme for conservation of Indian vultures has been started. There are various other similar programmes aimed towards conservation of biodiversity in the country. Together these are expected to contribute significantly in ex situ conservation of biodiversity in the country.

Traditional Knowledge Digital Library (TKDL): India is facing dangers from other countries in the form of biopiracy. Institutions and individuals in other countries have been regularly making efforts to obtain knowledge from India and obtain patents for them that the knowledge was created by them. Two famous cases related to *Neem* and *Haldi*. Patents were obtained in USA and Europe on medicinal properties of these two plants although therapeutic properties of these plants were known in India for very long time. The patents were challenged by Indian authorities. In case of *Haldi* (turmeric) the US authorities revoked the patent in 1997 and the decision proved to be a milestone. For the first time a patent which was based on traditional knowledge from a developing country was challenged and the judgment was in favour of the developing country. The patent related to Neem was revoked in 2000 as certain individuals and an NGO from India challenged the patent. Also, Basmati and *Terminalia arjun* (*Arjun*) were saved from being patented through similar initiatives. But these successes came at huge legal cost and wastage of time. Now things have become much easier. It has happened so on account of a unique initiative called Traditional Knowledge Digital Library (TKDL). Under TKDL about 219000 formulations of *Ayurveda, Siddha, Unani* and *Yoga* have been documented. The information is spread on 34 million pages in the form of a computer database. The task took more than 10 years to complete. TKDL is available in five languages i.e. English, French, German, Japanese and Spanish. The information included in TKDL was taken out from large number of documents in various languages including Arabic, Persian, Sanskrit, Tamil and Urdu. TKDL is being managed by CSIR (Council of Scientific and Industrial Research).

Because of TKDL, foreign patent offices have been able to settle cases in favour of India within two to ten weeks and without any cost. However, even now large numbers of patents related to the Indian systems of medicines are granted in USA and Europe. To take care of these issues Indian government is planning to sign agreements with different patent offices. These agreements will provide access to the patent offices to TKDL and they can check if the information is already listed in TKDL. In such cases patent has to be denied. Agreement with EPO (European Patent Office) was signed in February 2009 and with US Patent & Trademark Office (USPTO) in November 2009. The EPO has identified more than 35 cases using TKDL. Eight cases have been resolved in favour of India. Other cases were in process. USPTO has cited 40 cases of similar nature. Thus TKDL is proving very useful in protecting the Indian heritage from piracy.

Various awards and fellowships are in place to help in study and conservation of environment, including biodiversity. Indira Gandhi Paryavaran Puraskar is one, National Award for Prevention of Pollution is another, Rajiv Gandhi Environment Award for Clean Technology, Indira Priyadarshani Vrikshmitra Award, B.P. Pal National Environment Fellowship Award for Biodiversity, Pitambar Pant National Environment Fellowship are few more examples. These awards and prizes are given to deserving persons and organizations for distinctive contributions in the concerned fields. Directly and indirectly these are helping in conservation of biodiversity in the country.

□□□

CHAPTER 11

Future Scenario

Conservation of biodiversity has to be done on long term basis. To meet this goal it is essential that the development process and priorities are oriented in such a way that ecological security and livelihood issues are given due importance. Livelihood issues can be addressed if the community rights are ensured and national, international and local interests are properly balanced. Interest of the local community has to receive priority over national and international interests. Only then the local communities may be expected to be interested in protecting and conserving the biodiversity. One more aspect which is of importance is that poverty stricken people in any locality cannot be expected to protect the biological diversity. Their first priority will always be survival, even if it requires sacrifice of the ecosystems and biodiversity. They may behave to fell trees, harvest edible parts of plants or hunt animals for their survival. Hence, it is essential that poverty is addressed and eliminated and an acceptable standard of living is provided to one and all in the community and society.

To conserve and protect the biodiversity it may become essential to expand, strengthen and rationalize the network of Protected areas including those of national parks, wildlife Sanctuaries and biosphere reserves etc. Such initiatives may demand sacrifice in different forms from people inhabiting the area as they may have to restrict their activities. To take care of the possible resistance by people who will be affected, necessary measures have to be adopted. An important aspect is provision of alternate sources of income to compensate for restrictions on exploitation of resources from protected areas. Making provision for alternate sources of income may demand outside funding. Provision for the same will be easier if actual value of protected areas is ascertained by including the element of ecosystem services the protected areas provide in addition to the well understood service of providing safe sanctuary to the biodiversity. For example, the amount of ground water recharge that comes from there, the amount of oxygen they add to the atmosphere, the role they play in hydrological cycle, purification of the atmosphere, nutrient recycling etc. We have discussed this aspect in detail earlier. Also, we have seen how important these are in monetary term. Tourism to high biodiversity areas must be regulated strictly. Only genuine eco-tourism should be allowed in those areas. Local communities who have stake in protecting the biodiversity must be involved in management of tourism activity. Such involvement will enhance their income and also their interest in long-term survival of the biodiversity. Areas with high biodiversity should be kept away from developmental activities which may endanger biodiversity. In case of species which are endangered and their conservation is not possible in-situ, efforts should be made to protect them ex-situ. In-situ means in the habitat where the organism lives naturally. Ex-situ means at some site other than the natural habitat. For example, forest is the natural habitat for wild animals, plants etc. So, first preference should be to conserve the wild organisms in the forest itself. However, if it is impossible, they may be kept at some other suitable site. Botanical gardens, zoos, aquariums etc. are the possible alternatives. These areas and facilities can play important role in ex-situ conservation. Once if the conditions in the natural habitats turn favourable, the plants and animals can be reintroduced there.

As already discussed, conservation activities are not possible without the active involvement of the community. To ensure involvement of the community it is essential that livelihoods issues are given due importance. For example a large number of artisan activities are based on natural resources obtained from biodiversity. If such activities are encouraged, the community will be more interested in conserving those resources as they will be interested in long term availability of the resources. Similarly, medicinal plants are an important resource for large percentage of population in our country and in various other countries. It is estimated that about 15000 species of plants in the country have medicinal properties. About 8000 species of medicinal plants are in use in the country. Most species are used in folk tradition of medicine and health care. The medicinal plants are also used at family level and community level for day to day health problems and also for earning income through sale of the plants and products. However, in the present set up the actual collectors and growers get little benefit while the middle men, traders and manufacturers get maximum profit. This leads to a situation where collectors of medicinal plants have nothing much to lose if the resource vanishes. On the other hand, if the collection and sale of medicinal plants are properly organized so that the benefits flow to the community, the community will certainly be interested in conserving the resource to get permanent or at least long term benefits. Similar is the case with natural dyes and pigments. On the one hand these have to compete with cheap synthetic chemicals and on the other side the actual growers and processors get meager return. Major chunk of income is cornered by traders and middle men. There are instances when the collector or grower is given only ten rupees while those who take the same material to the markets in the country get two hundred rupees or even more and if the same item is exported, margin of profit for the traders and exporters rise many fold. In 2004, a new initiative was started by the Andaman & Nicobar Administration to produce pearls using Pearl Oysters Surgery. It was expected that the project could provide employment in a big way and also it was environment-friendly. The initiative has the potential to boost the economy and well being of the islanders. In return the community will be interested in protecting the coastal environment from pollution and degradation so that pearl culture continues unhindered. The same will benefit the environment and allow the rich biodiversity of the island to flourish.

Protection of Delhi Ridge by fencing. The Ridge was being encroached by different agencies and individuals. Supreme Court of India had to intervene to protect the Ridge on the initiative of citizens.

People make these mud structures on house tops in Egypt with holes and wood poles attached. Birds are provided with food in these structures. Migratory birds settle in these structures during transit.

Several varieties of Banana in a shop. An example of range of biodiversity in a single species.

A spider which preys upon harmful insects – that is the circle of life

To achieve the goals of conservation and sustainable utilization, it is essential that level of awareness about biodiversity is increased. Quite often we do not attach importance to animals and plants which are found in our own vicinity. Spiders, lizards, birds, snakes etc. are common examples. In fact, most of us are unaware about the facts relating to animals which result in hate and their being killed without any reason. Misinformation about these animals is widespread. For example, there are only four or five kinds of snakes in our country which are poisonous. But, people kill all snakes as soon as they find them. Also, there is widespread myth that snakes take revenge. It is believed that if a person kills a snake, its partner will search for the person and kill the person. This is totally false perception. But, large numbers of snakes are killed for this reason. In 2010 a college in UP was vacated for this reason. A snake was killed and there was the rumour that the other snake was looking for the killer to take revenge. It is essential that we learn to recognize the four poisonous snakes, i.e., Krait, Cobra, Russell viper and Saw-scaled viper so that the remaining more than 200 types of snakes found in India may be allowed to live. These snakes play an important role in keeping balance in the ecosystems. The case of an animal, Caecilian is even more tragic. These are amphibians which are without limbs and tail. Also, they cannot perceive sound as these are without ear and mostly without eyes as well. Only problem is that these animals move like snakes. Hence, people mistake them for snakes and kill them although they are totally harmless. Similar is the case of lizards. There is widespread misinformation that lizards are poisonous while the fact is that not even one species of lizard species found in India is poisonous. But, people kill them on account of false notion.

It has been reported that traditional drums, ghumats, used on Ganesh Chaturthi apparently spell doom for the Monitor Lizard, killed for the membranous surface. Although there are no figures available for the number of lizards sacrificed for this annually, some conservationists expect that it must be much wider than we realize.

Hindustan Times, New Delhi, August 2, 2004

Note: Killing of Monitor Lizard is banned under the Wildlife Protection Act, 1972. It is a punishable offence.

Regarding spiders there is misinformation that they are inauspicious. Also, people have the wrong notion that spiders are poisonous. So, people burn their webs and also kill them. Tarantulas are a special kind of spiders, which are large in size and look fiery. They hunt at night by running down their prey. They prey upon insects of different variety and also small mammals. Few Tarantulas are found in India. Luckily, these species are not poisonous enough to cause harm to humans. Still, people kill them thinking that they are poisonous. Reason is that several types of Tarantulas found in other countries are poisonous. In fact the spiders are very good insect killers. A very important issue is that the spiders live and hunt in remote corners where killing the insect pests otherwise is almost impossible. In case of birds too there are such examples. Vultures and owls are considered inauspicious in several regions of the country. As a result these are killed and their nests are destroyed. We have discussed about the other dangers being faced by these two types of birds in other Chapters. Together these activities are pushing these birds towards extinction. Even sparrows are on decline. There are various reasons to that. One important reason is that in past people did not mind if sparrows nested inside the house on lofts, ledges etc. Today they are denied that privilege on account of changes in house design and also because we do not like these birds to nest in our homes. Also, there is the misconception that sparrows are responsible for destruction of crops. We have discussed about this misconception and consequent killing of sparrows in China in an earlier chapter.

The facts about all these animals and birds are totally different. Snakes prey upon rats and mice, which destroy the standing crops and also the stored grains on very large scale. Lizards of all varieties prey upon insects and clean our environment from insects including those ones, which are responsible for spreading diseases. Similarly, the complete life cycle of spiders revolve round insects. Some of them hunt the insects directly while others make webs to trap insects. If we work out the contribution made by spiders in our own country in keeping the insects under control, it would run into billions of rupees per annum. Most of the birds which are found around us prey upon insects and small vermin. There are others like crows, vultures etc. which work as scavengers feeding upon the dead carcasses. In the process they keep our environment clean and healthy. Large numbers of plant species which are found around us yield edible products while others are of medicinal value. Still others provide food to birds and animals. Most of them provide safe habitat to birds, insects and also large animals. Irrespective of their size and other characters, all plants are soil binders and also play crucial role in enriching the soil with nutrients and in continuation of hydrological cycle. Hence, there is need to spread awareness and remove misinformation. This can be done through interaction, tourism, use of different media etc.

It may surprise a person who is not from Delhi, that Delhi has a dense forest right inside the city. It is the Delhi Ridge. This forest is an extension of the Aravalli range, and it is spread over about 7800 ha. Basically, it is a semi-arid scrub type of forest. Part of the Ridge is natural forest while the rest is the result of plantations made from middle of 19th century. This is the reason that flora of the Ridge comprises of natural vegetation as well as introduced species.

Till few decades back, Blue bull, Hog deer, Chinkara, Blackbuck, Fox, Jackal etc. were commonly found in the area. Occasionally, leopards have also been spotted in the forest. Occasionally, leopards have strayed out of the Ridge and entered the city. Efforts are made to capture the animal live. However, on certain occasions the animals get killed in the process. As far as smaller animals are concerned, these can be easily seen in the Ridge in large numbers.

The Ridge ecosystem is very rich in bird population. Certain reports suggest the presence of more than 200 species of birds in the area. This is the reason that bird watchers in large number throng the area.

On account of ecosystem degradation and occasional deaths in accidents on roads passing through the Ridge, population of larger animals in the Ridge has been reduced drastically. There are several main roads crossing the Ridge area. Also, there has been large scale encroachment of the Ridge on account of expanding city limits and high premium on land in Delhi. The lax government machinery always looked the other way for one reason or the other. All these aberrations resulted in elimination of biodiversity of the area to a great extent and by the last quarter of last century, it was being apprehended that the Ridge could be wiped out soon. However, in 1979, a students and citizens group took up the issue. By 1996, the pressure on administration was so much that they had to declare the Ridge a Reserve forest and on the orders of the Hon'ble Supreme Court, many encroachments were removed from the Ridge. As a result, construction in the Ridge area and also encroachments by individuals and organizations has been controlled to a large extent. With these initiatives, it is expected that this unique ecosystem will survive to provide the city of Delhi with fresh air and also help in recharging the ground water table on permanent basis. Most importantly, this unique ecosystem will act as a repository of distinct type of biodiversity right inside the city of Delhi.

We need to appreciate that apart from direct conservation of biodiversity, various other environment friendly initiatives can help conserve biodiversity. We must remember the three 'Rs' (Reduce, Reuse and Recycle). Reduction in consumption, reuse of resources and recycling of materials can also help conservation of biodiversity. Let us take one or two examples. We use water in our day to day activities. If we reduce its consumption by controlling wastage, our demand for water can come down to a great extent. This will reduce pressure from water sources. Further, the quantity of effluent or sewage that is generated will come down. As a result, treatment of waste water can be done more efficiently and the water bodies which presently receive large quantities of untreated or partially treated sewage or effluent will improve leading to better aquatic environment. This will certainly favour biodiversity associated with water bodies. If we reuse or recycle, water, the same results can be achieved. We regularly use paper in day to day life. If we reduce its consumption, it would mean less number of trees cut for pulp, less quantity of water used for production of paper, reduced quantum of effluent from paper mills, less consumption of chemicals, electricity etc. at the mill and less consumption of fuel to transport the paper and the waste paper produced. At the end the environment will improve and it will have positive impact on biodiversity. If we recycle or reuse paper, it will reduce demand for pulp, energy, water, chemicals etc. and also less of garbage will be generated. Paper recycling needs much less energy and water as compared to production of paper from raw materials. If we adopt these initiatives, the environment will be better and also the biodiversity will get boost.

The educational and awareness activities should target every section of the society, especially those who are in a position to take decisions. For example, when we plan to increase agricultural production, we should not be totally obsessed about use of chemical fertilizers, pesticides, monoculture etc. We must assess the impact vis-a- vis the biodiversity of the area and their long term implications. Similarly, it is essential to expand the irrigation potential and power generation for our growing needs. However, before planning any dam, hydro power plant, thermal power plant etc. it is essential that we must take into account the implications with respect to damage and loss to biodiversity. Biodiversity must also be assigned its due value and the same should be taken into account while performing the cost benefit analysis of the project. These are possible only when our policy makers, planners and administrators are sufficiently conscious about the value of biodiversity. They should not consider a tract of forest only as few hundred or few thousand trees. They should be in a position to appreciate that a forest does not mean only trees. It includes large and small animals, birds, insects, soil microorganisms, herbs, shrubs, climbers, lichens, orchids and so on. Also, they must evaluate the contributions made by the trees, other plants and various other organisms in different ways and add the same to the cost in the balance sheet as those services will disappear once the biodiversity is finished. However, the exercise should not be aimed to stall the developmental activities and projects. The purpose should be to help the decision makers to reach a conscious decision one way or the other. A large number of examples can be cited where fragmentation of natural forests and even protected areas have taken place due to developmental activities. Such fragmentations have resulted in loss of vegetation and also created problems for animals. For example, we know that elephants require migration corridors. If the corridors are disturbed, these animals get emotionally and physically disturbed. As a result, they attack humans and properties. Increasing number of instances of elephant human conflict has brought this problem to the fore. Mostly the elephants are killed people. At times humans are also killed or injured. Net result is that people develop hatred for the elephants without realizing that the animals are not at fault. Diversion of forest land for urbanization, laying of railway tracks or for expanding road network make wild animals vulnerable and they are killed on account of accidents or because of their straying into human settlements.

In the race to have more land in urban areas, large number of lakes, ponds and other water bodies have been systematically 'killed'. Result is that most of our cities and towns suffer from water scarcity. Historically, ponds, lakes, rivers etc. were revered in the country. Ponds attached to temples and 'mazaars' (mausoleum of saints) were highly respected. Similarly, rivers were given the status of mother and god. Hence, these were not used to dump wastes. But, recent wave of materialism has eliminated these feelings and people do not have the same reverence and respect for the water bodies. Most of our rivers are polluted and the population of fish and other animals has gone down drastically. People must be made aware of the biodiversity value and the important role played by the water bodies in hydrological cycle. It is possible that once they are informed, they will like to protect the water bodies. For example, a conscious and well informed town planner or administrator will think twice before suggesting that 'malbaa' or wastes be dumped in a pond, lake, estuary or coastal zone to 'create' more land. A telling example is of a wetland in the city of Chennai. Till recently, it was being used to dump municipal waste and it was slowly dying. Now, it is a protected wetland under the control of Forest Department.

Convention on Biological Diversity

If we look into the history of environmental conservation, we find that in 1992, the largest number of world leaders gathered in Rio de Janeiro, Brazil. The occasion was the United Nations Conference on Environment and Development. The Conference was organized on completion of twenty years of the path breaking conference at Stockholm in 1972. Although the 1972 Conference did not attract many world leaders, it started the process of renewed thinking about environmental conservation at global level. In 1992 several agreements were signed at the "Earth Summit". The agreements included two binding agreements, the Convention on Climate Change and the **Convention on Biological Diversity (CBD). CBD** was the first global agreement relating to the conservation and sustainable use of biological diversity. The **CBD** gained rapid and widespread acceptance. Over 150 governments signed the document during the Rio conference itself. So, far 193 nations have already signed the convention with one important exception i.e. USA. India was one of the early signatories.

The Convention has three important goals:

1. Conservation of biodiversity,
2. Sustainable use of various components of biodiversity,
3. Sharing of the benefits in a fair and equitable way. The benefits refer to the ones accruing from commercial and other uses of the genetic resources present in the form of biodiversity.

The Convention deals with an important issue which is vital to the survival and well being of human race. That is the reason that it now stands as a landmark in international law. It recognizes that the conservation of biological diversity is a concern of the entire human race and it must be made an integral part of all the developmental process. The CBD covers all ecosystems, species, and genetic resources present on Earth. The Convention attaches due importance to traditional conservation efforts along with the economic goal of using biological diversity in sustainable manner. It also sets guidelines for equitable sharing of the benefits originating from the use of genetic resources in the form of biodiversity, especially for commercial gains. The Convention also covers biotechnology aspects. It includes technology development and transfer, benefit-sharing and also bio-safety aspects. Most important feature of the Convention is that it is legally binding. Countries joining it are obliged to implement it. The Convention functions under the aegis of the United Nations.

The Convention offers decision-makers guidance based on precautionary principles. Where there is threat of significant reduction or loss of biological diversity, lack of full scientific certainty should not be used as a reason or excuse for postponing measures to reduce or avoid the threat. The Convention makes it clear that substantial investments are essential to conserve biological diversity. Then it further elucidates that biodiversity conservation will bring significant environmental, economic and social benefits in return. The Convention also emphasizes on ecological, genetic, social, economic, scientific, educational, cultural, recreational and aesthetic values of biological diversity and its components. Hence the investments made in conservation of biodiversity will bring adequate return in several ways.

Then the Convention affirms that conservation of biological diversity should be a common concern of humankind and that the States have sovereign rights over the biological resources present in their territory and the States are responsible for conserving their biological diversity and for using their biological diversity resources in a sustainable manner.

The Convention also suggests steps to plan and implement appropriate measures to develop scientific, technical and institutional capacities to provide the basic understanding which can help save the biodiversity. The same has been provided as the Convention has recognized that the biological diversity is eroding significantly on account of certain human activities. Also, it has been accepted that there is general lack of information and knowledge regarding biological diversity and its importance which is resulting in neglect towards the biodiversity.

The Convention then recognizes the importance of anticipation, prevention and recognition of the causes of significant reduction or loss of biodiversity at source. The convention also identifies that fundamental requirement for the conservation of biological diversity is the in-situ conservation of ecosystems and natural habitats and the maintenance and recovery of viable populations of species in their natural surroundings. As a compromise it acknowledges that ex-situ measures also have an important role to play. However, it clarifies that such measures should preferably be in the country of origin of the organisms concerned.

The Convention recognizes the close dependence of many indigenous and local communities leading traditional lifestyles on biological resources. Those communities have wealth of traditional knowledge accumulated over centuries. The traditional knowledge may prove of great help to the modern society and different types of benefits may accrue in the process. The Convention admits that conservation and sustainable use of biological diversity is very important for meeting the food, health and other needs of the expanding world population. Hence, it accepts that access to and sharing of both genetic resources and technologies are essential to meet these goals. The Convention duly emphasizes upon the desirability of equitable sharing of benefits arising from the use of traditional knowledge and also innovations and practices relevant to the conservation of biological diversity and its sustainable use. It then stresses upon the need to promote international, regional and global cooperation among States and inter-governmental organizations and the non-governmental sector for the conservation of biological diversity and its sustainable utilization.

Certain objectives have also been identified for the Convention. It includes conservation of biological diversity, sustainable use of its components and fair and equitable sharing of the benefits arising out of the utilization of genetic resources.

Thus, the Convention which has been signed by most of the nations except USA came into force on 29th December 1993. As it can be seen from the above, it recognizes in clear terms the importance of biodiversity, its role in human welfare and its value for the society and it suggests suitable measures to be adopted for conservation and sustainable utilization of the same. India is one of the signatories to the Convention. Hence, apart from our own benefit, we also have an international obligation to protect the bio-diversity present in our country.

Taking the same into consideration, the **Biological Diversity Act, 2002** was enacted on 5th February, 2003.

The legislation primarily addresses the issues concerning access to biological resources and associated knowledge by foreign individuals, institutions, or companies and equitable sharing of benefits arising out of the use of the biological resources and knowledge with the country and the people.

Salient Features of the Legislation

The main intent of this legislation is to protect India's rich biodiversity and associated knowledge against their use by foreign individuals and organizations without sharing the benefits arising out of such use, and to check biopiracy. The Act provided for setting up of a National Biodiversity Authority (NBA), State Biodiversity Boards (SBBs) and Biodiversity Management Committees (BMCs) in local bodies. NBA and SBB are required to consult BMCs in decisions relating to use of biological resources/related knowledge within their jurisdiction and BMCs are to promote conservation, sustainable use and documentation of biodiversity.

All foreign nationals/organizations require prior approval of NBA for obtaining biological resources and/or associated knowledge for any use. Indian individuals/entities require approval of NBA for transferring results of research with respect to any biological resources to foreign nationals/organizations. Collaborative research projects are permissible and exchange of knowledge and resources under these projects are exempted provided they are drawn as per the policy guidelines of the Central Government and have its approval.

Indian industry is required to give prior intimation to the concerned SBB about obtaining any biological resource for commercial use, and the SBB may restrict the activity if found to violate the objectives of conservation, sustainable use and benefit sharing. However, Indian citizens/entities/local people including "vaids" and "hakims" have free access to use biological resources within the country for their own use, medicinal purposes and research purposes. While granting approvals, NBA can impose terms and conditions to secure equitable sharing of benefits. Before applying for any form of IPRs in or outside India for an invention based on research or information on biological resource obtained from India, prior approval of NBA will be required. There is an enabling provision for setting up a framework for protecting traditional knowledge. The monetary benefits, fees, royalties as a result of approvals by NBA are to be deposited in National Biodiversity Fund which will be used for conservation and development of areas from where resource has been accessed. The same is to be done in consultation with the concerned local self government.

Also, there is provision for notifying National Heritage Sites from stand point of biodiversity. The same can be done by State Governments in consultation with concerned local self-governments. Also, there is provision for notifying items, areas for exemption, provided such exclusion does not violate other provisions. This provision has been kept to exempt normally traded commodities so as not to adversely affect day to day trade. Thus it is expected that in future biodiversity present in different parts of the world will remain safe and will be utilized in a sustainable manner keeping in view the different provisions of the CBD.

Table 1 : Aerial Extents of Some Coastal Marine Ecosystems in India

S.No.	*Ecosystem type*	*Area (Km²)*
1.	Estuaries	1540
2.	Lagoons	1564
3.	Creeks	192
4.	Backwater	171
5.	Tidal/Mud flat	23621
6.	Coral Reefs	2330
7.	Mangroves	3401
8.	Sandy beaches/bars/spits	4210
9.	Rocky coasts	177
10.	Slat Marshes	1698
11.	Salt Pans	655
12.	Aquaculture ponds	769
13.	Other Vegetation	1391

Table 2 : Recorded No. of Plant Species in the World and in India

Group	*World*	*India*	*Percentage*
Bacteria/Viruses	8,050	903	11.2
Algae	40,000	7,182	17.9
Fungi	72,000	14,588	20.2
Lichens	13,500	2,268	16.8
Bryophytes	16,600	2,451	14.7
Pteridophytes	10,000	1,236	12.3
Gymnosperms	650	69	10.6
Angiosperms	250,000	17,643	7.00
Total	**410,800**	**46,340**	**11.2**

Table 3 :Estimated Numbers of Faunal Species, Globally and in India

Taxonomic Group	*No. of Species*		*Percentage in India*
	India	*World*	
Protista (Protozoa)	31250	3277	10.49
Arthropoda	970670	69903	07.20
Chordata	48451	5085	10.50
Protochordata	2106	119	05.65
Pisces	21723	2556	11.77
Amphibia	5150	310	06.02
Reptilia	5817	466	08.01
Aves	9026	1232	13.66
Mammalia	4629	402	08.68
Total (Animalia)	1191208	88981	7.47
Grand Total (Protista + Animalia)	1222458	92258	7.55

Index